BURMAH

LETTERS AND PAPERS

WRITTEN IN 1852–53

BY

MAJOR-GENERAL HENRY GODWIN

LATE COMMANDING IN BURMAH
ARRACAN AND TENASSERIM

The Naval & Military Press Ltd

Reproduced by kind permission of the Central Library,
Royal Military Academy, Sandhurst

Published by
The Naval & Military Press Ltd
Unit 10, Ridgewood Industrial Park,
Uckfield, East Sussex,
TN22 5QE England
Tel: +44 (0) 1825 749494
Fax: +44 (0) 1825 765701
www.naval-military-press.com

© The Naval & Military Press Ltd 2004

In reprinting in facsimile from the original, any imperfections are inevitably reproduced and the quality may fall short of modern type and cartographic standards.

THE BURMESE WAR.

PREFACE.

THE family and friends of the late General Godwin have felt anxious to see some short authentic statement which should relieve his memory from the many imputations, which portions of the press, both in England and India, so pertinaciously brought against him. But little hesitation could be entertained in complying with such a wish, inasmuch as General Godwin himself, very shortly before his death, had transmitted to this country (for insertion in certain leading journals) a statement in answer to the charges; that it was owing to his want of energy that the force employed in Burmah went into quarters at Rangoon; did not advance at once on Ava; as well as that it had been unnecessarily exposed and badly provisioned.

The insertion of the statement in question was not asked for, but some portions of it will be found in the following pages; and if others have been suppressed, it has been first, because though not in the least too strong to express a sense of personal injustice, they may be withheld when such a statement becomes a posthumous one; and because in some instances the original documents referred to have not yet been received.

The omissions from General Godwin's own statement have been made good by extracts from his correspondence with a near relative, and will be sufficient, perhaps, to show; what was the primary object which the Government of India contemplated when it despatched the force intrusted to him; and at how early a period that line of policy had been decided on which guided the Governor-General and Council in their dealings with the Court of Ava, when the capture of the cities along the sea-coast had failed to secure the hoped-for results.

The extracts from the letters extend over two years, and show an amount of service, with fatigue and exposure, cheerfully because easily endured, which will tend to correct the misrepresentations—that the officer selected to command was an "octogenarian general," "rendered inactive by age and infirmities." General Godwin was in his sixty-seventh year when he embarked for Burmah. A short account of his services in that country in the war of 1824 is appended, as it was on a consideration of those services that he was selected to command.

General Godwin had the ill-fortune to command in an unpopular war: not because, as it seemed to some, that the amount of injury sustained (without some superadded overbearing on our part) hardly afforded a sufficiency of offence to warrant aggression, but because, under partisan journalism, whatever is, is all well done, or is all wrong.

"There is a determination," General Godwin remarks, writing from Burmah, "to represent things here as they are not."

The Administration at home, under which, but not by which, hostilities with Burmah were brought on, had enough to do, and no time to spare for the things doing on the other side of the globe; and the Administration which succeeded accepted the results without troubling itself for those who had been concerned, or the injustice done them: on such chances and changes as these depends the good or evil service which a man's successes for others may do for himself. "Fate," says Defoe, "kicks some up stairs and some down—some are advanced without honour, others suppressed without infamy—some are raised without merit, some are crushed without crime; and no man knows by the beginning of things whether his course shall issue in a peerage or a pillory."

THE BURMESE WAR.

The following statement neither relates to the recent military operations in Burmah, nor yet to the policy by which those operations were undertaken and carried out. It is a personal one, relating only to my own position as the officer to whom was intrusted the command of the forces employed. During the continuance of that command, it would not have been proper that I should have remonstrated against any misrepresentations; the reasons for such forbearance no longer exist—that army is now broken up, and I am left free to address myself to them.

I am well aware that those in the public service of a free country are properly liable, and must expect the criticisms of the press; but every man has a right to truth and fair dealing. I have not met with these; nor have I had the support I ought to have had from those to whom the policy of the Government of India was perfectly well known, and by whom such support could have been easily given. I am, therefore, forced myself to expose the calumnies and accusations of which I have been the victim.

The public was always addressed on Burmese affairs as if the writers were perfectly conversant with the wishes, orders, and intentions of the Government. It will be seen that they know nothing whatever; and, moreover, that they were most deplorably ignorant of the country the army was acting in. If anxiety for the public service prompted the attacks, and required that I should be held up to odium, fair dealing required that I should have been exonerated by the same organs, when it had been made clear that I was not at fault. The printed papers relating to "Hostilities with Burmah" contained my complete vindication against every charge; yet, though the proofs were there, the tone of public criticism did not change, and I was as much the subject of offensively personal attacks as ever.

I was at Calcutta in November, 1851, on my way to Umballa to take the command of the Sirhind division. At that time the *Fox* frigate was there, and Commodore Lambert was then in treaty with the Council, on the subject of a visit to Rangoon to demand satisfaction for aggressions on the Resident and our traders there. I wrote a letter to the Commander-in-Chief respecting this Burmese difference, as I knew this people as well as any one then in India. I pointed out that half measures would not succeed with them, and that any demands upon them should be backed by the means of enforcing them: that with six regiments I would keep the whole of the Rangoon district; and that with ten thousand (half of what we had there before) I would go all over the country; and that the present (November) was the proper time.

By January, 1852, I had reached Umballa, and by that time Burmese affairs wore a very cloudy aspect—another war seemed imminent.

Umballa, February 19, 1852.

"We are now at war with Burmah, and I am deeply interested in the measures the Government may take; for, if an army is again exposed to the Ava monsoon, it will meet with the fate of the last.* I have written another letter to the Commander-in-Chief, and should like to command the force, should they send one; and if they wish to put a speedy end to the war, they will employ me. I say not this from any conceit, but from the plain, common-sense reason that I served so long against them—that I know the people and

---

* Of the force sent to Burmah under Sir Archibald Campbell in 1824, nearly 75 per cent. died.

their country, as well as their peculiar warfare and defences. Most in India think that I shall have it; but a large part of the force will go from Madras, and I am a long way up the country here. Whether or no, I think it fortunate that I am out here, for of all wars a Burmese one is most extravagant and difficult, from the circumstance that the country does not aid you in any one way.

"I have had a letter from the Commander-in-Chief to say that he had sent my letter 'on a Burmese war' to the Governor-General, and that he had reasons to know that no army would be sent to Ava till November; but that 'it would gratify the Governor-General to know from the best authority in India what was the right and only course to take in such a case.'"

On the evening of the 19th of February, an express reached me from the Commander-in-Chief, in consequence of one to him from the Governor-General, to hurry me to Calcutta for the purpose of considering operations against the Burmese—no hope now remaining of an accommodation with their Government, as one of our ships had been fired upon and a seaman killed.

Umballa, February 19, 1852.

"I shall start the day after to-morrow, and mean to travel day and night so as to reach Calcutta by the 1st or 2nd of March. What a strange thing that, having arrived in India so as to have been in time for the first Burmese war in 1824, I should have just reached it again for this important command! I am as well fitted for it by health and strength as ever I was, and it is impossible for me to say how gratified I am."

Calcutta, March 3, 1852.

"I arrived here yesterday, and am surprised at my own health and strength, though the journey down has taken the colour out of the cheeks of my young Aide-de-Camp. I was with the Governor-General to-day."

[This extract is given, as the attacks on General Godwin began before he was appointed to the command of the forces for Burmah. His *slow* journey down was one of the reasons assigned why the expedition was delayed.]

At my interview with the Governor-General, I learned that an expedition was preparing, to consist of H.M. 80th and two Native Regiments, with a company of Artillery, from Bengal; H.M. 51st Light Infantry, two Native Regiments, and two companies of Artillery, from Madras; and that I was to command. That there would be also Admiral Austen's flag-ship, 74; the *Fox*, 48; and several steamers. It has been asserted by those who pretended to know what passed at this interview, that I "debated and hesitated." It is true that certain parts of the proposed plan were not in accordance with my views, and I stated my objections firmly and honestly. These were, that if the proposed operations were to be the commencement of extended ones in that country, we were beginning at the wrong season, as the rains would come on in May; that if it was only proposed to go and destroy what we might, we should not influence the Government of Ava, as it possessed no public establishments; that what we should destroy would soon be put up again; that by leaving the country, and returning again in case the first demonstration failed to produce the desired results, we should have to do all over again in October, and that such a proceeding would greatly increase the expense, as well as destroy the unity and dignity of our proceedings. The Governor-General listened attentively, and replied that he was quite prepared for all I said, but that public opinion expected something of a strong nature, as all conciliatory measures had failed; and so the thing was determined on. The charge is a false one which imputed to me that I had "damped and chilled the promptness and vigour of the councils of the Governor-General."

Government House, Calcutta, March 14, 1852.

"I am gazetted to the command of the Forces to be employed in Burmah, as well as those in our own adjacent provinces, and expect to leave about the 23rd. The rendezvous is at the mouth of the Rangoon river; but I think that I shall be at Moulmein a few days before that, to see to the reduction of Martaban, which, I think, will open the drama.

"The King of Ava has been allowed until the 1st of April to make up his mind whether to pay indemnities and make certain concessions, or abide the consequences. Our first demand was 900 rupees (£90); now it is ten lacs (£100,000). This beats the Sybil's terms hollow. I feel no doubt whatever but that he will refuse the payment and try his strength. *The operations at Rangoon are to be considered as all that can be done before the rains.* I may try and get up to Prome before the monsoon, by the aid of steam-power; but this will depend on the capability of the river to receive the steamers at this season of the year, when the waters are at their lowest. There will also be the state of health of our men after the first operations, when fever and dysentery are sure to show themselves; the garrisons we may require, from the numbers and disposition of the Burmese, of which as yet we know nothing. Should their force be considerable and offensive, it would not do to jump over their heads, for the certainty of having to jump back again the moment any garrison was threatened. Rather than this, my policy would be, to beat them in the field, and drive them before me, so as to leave the population of the country (free) to be able to declare itself without risk, and become our friends, which it never could do by a jump of this sort. All this is mere speculation, though such a move may be; if not, I shall have to pass another monsoon at Rangoon, though certainly under very different circumstances to the last (1824). The care and provision which has been made to enable us to meet the rains is, I may say, parental. There are to be bake-houses; a constant supply of fresh meat; hospitals at Amherst to relieve me, to which the sick are to be carried round. *The only difficulty I ever felt respecting the occupation of Rangoon at the setting in of the rains was, as to cover for the men.* But hundreds of skeleton houses are now, and for some time have been making at Moulmein; so that, contrary to my first impression, I have great hopes that, if we cannot go on, we shall be able to hold the ground we shall have taken, without the losses we met with before from exposure and bad food."

In my communication with the Governor-General at this time, my opinions respecting the course to be adopted towards Burmah in case we entered on a war were such as I had held ever since the war of 1824—namely, that we should repair the mistake we then made, in not taking the kingdom of Pegue; that such should be the object of any renewed hostilities, and that they should be undertaken, as to time and manner, so that we might be there at the best season, and that the operations might not be protracted. From my knowledge of this people, and the nature of the Government, I did not think that any blow would have the desired effect of making them accept our terms.

Government House, Calcutta, March.

" Should the contemplated expedition ultimately force the Government to take possession of Burmah, I am to have a fine force of 14,000, composed of the best materials, which will be preparing during the rains, and ready to leave Rangoon in October. With this there will be a noble steam-power; so that my progress will be quiet and steady, and with everything with me that I could wish. I have an excellent Staff and Medical Department, a Military Secretary, and two Aides-de-Camps. My Adjutant-General, the best in this country, the Quartermaster-General, the Judge-Advocate, the Commanding Officer of Artillery, are given to Madras. In myself I am confident, without presumption. I shall leave nothing to chance, but in all things so act as never to be the victim of surprise; and I start with what no other officer in India could—a thorough knowledge of the country and its people. My health, thank God! is something wonderful, considering the impressions people have of India, and yet I have hardly had any rest—I have travelled out to India, then over 2,300 miles of ground, and slept in my clothes twenty-eight nights."

Government House, Calcutta, March 18, 1852.

"I had a letter from Commodore Lambert, from the Rangoon river, last night, saying, amongst other things, that the works about the Town were strong as numerous. I have an excellent plan of the whole. I am, as you may well suppose, a good deal occupied, as every department is busy with this armament, particularly the Ordnance. I can now say that all will be ready by the 25th; and after that, our leaving will depend on the Government. If on my arrival at the Rangoon river, I find that the force is not assembled, my intention is to go to Moulmein, and see to Martaban; but if all be ready, I shall proceed to Rangoon, respecting which my arrangements are made with the Commodore, and settle all there. I could have wished to have done all this by going earlier; but our hands are tied by having given them till the 1st of April for accepting our terms. I shall be glad when I am off, as then no change of any sort can take place."

Government House, Calcutta, March 21, 1852.

"I have just come up from a long conversation with the Governor-General, and I am more than ever satisfied with my position. . . . His Lordship said, 'I intend to leave you a free agent in the Civil Department, to make a peace, under your instructions, in such way as may appear to you best, knowing the people and country as you do; so you will have no control, nor did I ever intend that you should, depending on your management in every way with perfect confidence.'"

My private instructions, dated the 24th of March, are given among the printed papers. They were as follows:—

" Should a letter have come down from the Court of Ava, I was to ascertain its contents; and should it accede to the demands of the British Government, I should abstain from hostilities.

" Should the Court of Ava seem disposed to accede to our demands, as soon as practicable, I was to suspend hostilities, and treat in a fair and liberal spirit.

" Should there be no communication from the Court of Ava, or a direct refusal to accede, I was to proceed to act."

It was pointed out that operations would be most effectually directed against Martaban and Rangoon. The views of the Government are explicitly stated as follows:—

"*The Governor-General in Council has directed the assembling of this force in hope that a powerful blow struck promptly now may reduce the Burmese to reason; may obtain compliance with our demands, and so may avert the necessity for war upon a more extended scale, after the close of the coming monsoon.*"

I embarked at Calcutta on the 26th of March, and arrived at the place of rendezvous on the 2nd of April. In accordance with my instructions, I sent Captain Latter, under a flag of truce, to inquire whether any communication had been received. On reaching the stockades the flag was fired on.

The Madras division had not made its appearance. I therefore determined to proceed at once to Moulmein. We left the Rangoon river at daybreak on the morning of the 3rd, and were at Moulmein by noon of the 4th. Orders were immediately issued for the embarkation of the troops at four P.M.; and by nine P.M. a wing of H.M. 18th, a wing of H.M. 80th, a wing of the 26th M.N.I., with detachments of Bengal Artillery and Madras Sappers, in all 1400 men, were on board. The arrangements for the attack on Martaban commenced at daybreak on the 5th, and by eight P.M. the place was won. For an account of this service I must refer to my report to the Secretary to Government, dated Moulmein, April 6th. The same day, Martaban received its garrison, and I returned to the Rangoon river by the 8th, where I found that the Madras division had arrived the day before; *so that no time had been lost by my going to Martaban.*

I was delighted with the position of Moulmein. Now that Martaban is ours, this place will be more considered, and a more comfortable residence. It lies exactly opposite Moulmein, about two hours' sail or row; and has now 60,000 inhabitants.

I have stated in my despatch from Rangoon of the 18th of April that the 9th of April was devoted to making every disposition for the landing of the troops, and to becoming acquainted with the heads of departments of the Madras division. I informed the Admiral, on the evening of that day, that my preparations were complete; and his Excellency proceeded up the river next day.

In the same despatch will be found a full account of the arduous and trying duties which devolved on the force I had the honour to command during the days of the 12th, 13th, and 14th of April; and which, thanks to the great energy, temper, and endurance exhibited, resulted in the capture of Rangoon.

Great Pagoda, Rangoon, April 15, 1852.

"I have just time for a few lines to say that, thank God! I am alive and well; but through more fire and sun than

I have had to encounter for many a year. The stake was a great one; but this fine force has shown such temper, courage, perseverance, and endurance, that we have accomplished all, and crippled the enemy by the loss of all their guns, and their enormous works here, on which they had depended for all their hopes of success in opposing us. My great object was to get the Great Pagoda; as I knew that, when that fell, all would follow. You will see by the papers what we did. I have been occupied a good deal, as I have had to tell my own story myself. The cheer of the storming-party (800 men), as we entered the Pagoda, was worth all the stars in Europe."

Rangoon, April 23.

"It is not yet a month since I left Calcutta. Lord Dalhousie accompanied me on board, and his parting was warm and kind, such as I have uniformly found him. I feel gratified at having fulfilled his hopes in despatching this armament; for our success has certainly been a 'heavy blow.' The strength of this place is astonishing to me. The storming into the Great Pagoda was a beautiful sight. The 800 men had to descend from a height, where a battery was (and where we lost a good many, the shots plunging in on us constantly); then to traverse a pretty valley to the ascent to the Pagoda. They marched through the battery, wound their way silent and steady, till they reached the foot of the rising ground on which the Pagoda stands. Then came the rush up it, under cannon and musketry. In a few minutes the shout told all. The men then spread out, and drove all before them. My reward was, and ever will be, in that loud huzza which all the regiments in the rear heard and understood. The support was ready to advance, and all were in in an hour.

"There have been losses and casualties which I have to

regret. Colonel Bogle asked to be with me at the capture of Martaban, which, of course, I assented to; but, unfortunately, when I was on the point of leaving Moulmein, to return to Rangoon, he requested that he might come with me. At the attack on the stockade, on our landing on Monday, I saw him near me; and all my wish, that he should keep out of the coming risk, was in vain: in five minutes I heard that he had been badly wounded through the thigh. He has charge of the Tenasserim Provinces, and is most important to us. He is preparing houses for this army, to cover it against the rains, and which I expect shortly, together with 500 men to erect them. His wound is a serious loss to me, in himself, though I have a host in my Engineer, Major Frazer, with twelve officers of that service to assist.

"The heat of this place is terrible just now; and you will read of its destruction on our force on the Monday of our landing. It staggered me once or twice to think how disastrously it might affect our operations. My constitution is wonderful; I hardly sat down from daybreak till seven in the evening. Five times I had to provide against the bold advance of their skirmishers on the camp, or, I should say, bivouac, for tents we had not. At eight o'clock I lay down, tired enough, and slept so soundly that I was not aware of having been rolled on to a bed made by my side, and which had been brought up for me from the frigate; I only woke with the *réveillé*. I constantly wore my cocked hat and plume, and I am sure that it guarded my head from the sun better than the common forage-cap covered with quilted calico, with a flap down the neck. They were three trying days for all of us. I was never absent from the advance: lived with it, and slept with it, and can speak to its cheerfulness and devotion.

"The life I am now leading is full of work and activity: after dressing by candle-light, I am on horseback at six.

I lay by as much as I *can* during the heat of the day. At eleven P.M. the different departments of the army are with me for two hours. I also hear all cases against spirit-dealers; for I have more fear of spirits getting into our quarters than either of the Burmese or of the sun. I have dealt with this so severely that I have put a stop to it, and before spirit-drinking had produced any ill-effects, for the conduct of this army is admirable. Then comes my public and private correspondence. I am again always on horseback at five P.M., seeing to the lines, inspecting some corps, &c., till seven, when I dine."

From the capture of Rangoon, I became the subject of more virulent abuse, reckless misrepresentation, and insulting comparisons, than ever before assailed one in my position, even when unsuccessful; and my support under which was, that I had received the approval of those I had served, and earned the confidence of those I commanded. Our relations with Burmah in the month of May, 1852, were simply as follows : our force had not been sent against Ava, nor even for the subjugation of a single province; the nature of our difference would not have authorised any such aggression. The dismemberment of Burmah, if destined to take place, was to be the result of the courses of its own Government. A pecuniary loss had been sustained, and a pecuniary compensation had been required. Should such a demand be refused, the capture of Martaban and Rangoon had been considered a likely means of forcing compliance; and the effect of such a proceeding on our part would, it was thought, be improved by the vigour and readiness of the blow.

Rangoon, April.

"I have received the thanks and observations of the Governor-General in Council on my operations—they are most flattering. A salute was ordered at every station in India. In his private letter to me he says, 'You have prefaced a brilliant service. Your success has been uninterrupted and complete. I will not say that you have exceeded my expectations, because, after I had the pleasure of knowing you, I anticipated the result which your judgment, capacity, and resolution have effected; and I can sincerely say that it is impossible for any one to be personally and officially more satisfied with, and gratified by a public service than I have been by that which you have just rendered to our country.' He ends his letter, which has reference to many subjects, by saying, 'Now, fare-you-well for the present! Do not expose yourself needlessly, and believe me, &c.'

"The public General Order, dated Fort William, February 28th, 1852, says, 'The Governor-General in Council has had the satisfaction of publishing, for general information, despatches which announce the success of the expedition in the capture of Martaban, in the destruction of the formidable defences along the river, and in the assault and occupation of the fortifications of Rangoon.

"'The Governor-General in Council cannot employ terms too strong in expressing his unqualified approbation of the brilliant service which has thus been performed, and his gratitude to those by whose joint exertions it has been achieved.

"'His admiration is due equally to the perfect cordiality and concert with which Navy and Army have acted together; to the gallantry which has been conspicuous in the field; and to the fortitude and patience with which all have endured, without a murmur, a fierceness of climate, whose deadly influence is, unhappily, too well attested by the number of those who have fallen victims to its effects.

"'The Governor-General in Council especially desires to offer to the Commander-in-Chief of H.M. Naval Forces in these seas his warm acknowledgment of the ready co-operation, and of the very effective aid which his Excellency has afforded to the Government of India by the powerful squadron under his command, whose operations he has so ably directed, and in whose services he has borne so distinguished a part.

"'To Lieutenant-General Godwin, commanding the forces in Ava, the Governor-General in Council begs leave to tender his most full and cordial thanks for the manner in which, by his intrepidity, his energy and ability, he has brought the military operations of the force to their present successful issue; and to congratulate him upon thus having won fresh and higher honours upon the same scene on which he formerly gained so much distinction.'

"What all this may mean never gives me a moment's thought. India is always producing sudden changes; and what an extraordinary change in position is mine! But two months since I was living quietly in Upper India; since then I have done some good service, and at the head of a beautiful force of 7000 men, *and good ones*. I strongly suspect that the Burmese will play the same game as before, and try the effect the monsoon will have upon us. The country of Pegue, south of Prome, would be ours by a single word; but I never allow any prospect of this sort to be held out, as the penalty would be sad, should we leave them. All the country round is friendly to us; and we have hundreds of the people working here daily, and who are fairly, I may say, well paid. There is an enormous population outside the walls, and a great many inside. I shall allow them a few weeks; and if no offer come down from the Government, I shall make up my mind to be a year in this country, though I should be rejoiced to make a peace—it would be equal to another success, and would relieve the Government of a heavy expense; though this war is not costing one-tenth what the former one did. The damp is very great now, owing to the rains; bowel complaints are prevalent, but as yet no fever and no cholera. There is plenty to eat; the arrangements made by Lord Dalhousie are most excellent: nothing has been forgotten."

Rangoon, May 26, 1852.

"I have only time to say that I am well; my despatches will show what I have been about. My absence has thrown much work on me; and this, together with my despatches, which, with all their faults, I write myself, has taken up every hour. I have given up all ideas that we shall receive any propositions for a peace; they will wait and see whether the rains will kill us as before, not knowing that we are now nobly off. The vast population of this place is an extraordinary sight to contemplate. The Pegue district is ours in feeling; and it is to be regretted that it is not annexed, and so made an end to the war in the beginning, as they must annex, I foresee, in the end. It is with the Burmese of the upper country, and with the Shaans, that we must fight."

Rangoon, May 29, 1852.

"My hurried note after my return from Bassein was inevitable—my pen was not out of my hand for three days. I have no Military Secretary, though the Governor-General is ever pressing me to have one. I had appointed my Adjutant-General at Umballa to this post; but, from his position, he could not join me (though Lord Dalhousie and Sir William Gomm had smoothed everything) before the first operations here, and I thought that I would wait and see what influence these might have on the Burmese, to make them sue for peace. Moreover, I have only one Aide-de-Camp (Chads) out of two, for the Commodore's son (Lambert) was obliged to go home. We are well in for the monsoon now. As to our future, it is as deep a mist to me as it is to you in England.

"You would have been delighted with the progress up that most beautiful river leading to Bassein; we ascended sixty miles before we came in sight of the city and its bright

Gold Pagoda. The banks are not high, the foliage beautiful, the tints on many of the trees like those of our beach in autumn. On the left, and near, forming a back-ground, are the fine hills of Arracan. The river is full of islands; the vegetation rich and varied, reaching to the water's edge, and drooping into it. The entrance into the estuary is at Diamond Island; you next reach Negrais Island, high and covered with verdure, and then commence the ascent of the river with its islands and creeks, which are pretty rivers in themselves.

"There is an enormous population around us here; they have large bazaars, where everything is to be had in abundance. How different from the last war of starvation!

"The troops are now in excellent health, and ready for any service. The population under our protection here is so large that their quiet conduct is a marvel to me. The women come about the quarters of the soldiers, up and down the lines with fruit for sale, in perfect confidence, showing the admirable state and conduct of this army.

"The rains do not seem to me to be so continuous as in the last war."

Rangoon, June 20, 1852.

"The authorities in India seem very well pleased. Sir William Gomm has issued an order on our doings, and has also addressed Lord Fitzroy Somerset at home for the information of the Duke. His private letter to me is so kind in feeling that it is a return beyond all honours. I feel and know that turning their works at Rangoon as we did was a soldier-like proceeding; had I attacked their tremendous Bund, I should, if not beaten back, have lost half my force.

"I have a most gentlemanly set of officers about me, and who are so perfectly acquainted with the duties of their several departments that I am very well off. I have now a good house, but it is frightfully damp. We are going to have private theatricals, which I was very glad to give in to; occupation and amusement are the great secrets of health at this season. The Bassein affair was a neat one. Lord Dalhousie told me that our work had been 'well rounded off.'

"We are here till the rains are over, and shall then be ready for an advance; and I will not halt, except to set aside Burmese opposition, till I reach the capital of this Empire, unless (as I fear they may) they come down and offer peace, when they see our fine force drawing on them. My mind is, however, made up on that point: the only act that shall stop me will be their bringing and laying the money at the head of my advance; this will be the only proof I will accept of their sincerity. I will have no sham peace-making, as we had in the last war, and by which we lost several weeks. As yet we have not had the slightest communication with the Court of Ava; all from 50 miles south of Prome up to Amerapoora is as yet sealed to us. I have been busy in considering and giving in to Government the nature and strength of the force I shall require, and which it has called for; the details are troublesome, the Commissariat most so of all. Should I be ordered to move, I shall be at the head of a fine force, with a water column on the Irrawaddy attending.

"The rains are going on, but the health of the men is improving, thanks to the foresight of the Governor-General, which has provided such excellent barracks, and everything the men can want."

Rangoon, July 17, 1852.

"I only returned a day or two since from Martaban and Bassein, where I went to see to the progress of the defences at both places, as well as to take the Chief Engineer, in order to prevent any errors, or want of caution. About a month since I was nearly on my way to Martaban, to take it for the third time, as it had a narrow escape of being recaptured by the Burmese; it is now pretty secure. I was eight days at sea, which has done me good.

"With respect to the malignant paragraphs of the *Times*, I cannot but think that they will serve rather than injure me, after my complete success in everything I have had to do. If I know anything of my own trade, the strong place we are now living in could not have been taken with less loss, nor more satisfactorily to the minds of the soldiers. A man in command in this country has, however, more than enough to bear up against, amid those who join with editors; personally I care for it as little perhaps as any man in my situation ever did: it never robs me of an hour's rest.

"Should we move, I hope to have a scientific man with us, and have begged of Lord Dalhousie to attach one to the force.

"Lord Dalhousie is coming here himself in a few days, I am happy to say, to arrange as to our advance, &c. I hope that they will do something at home, and brevet the officers recommended for good conduct, and in command during the three days at Rangoon. I see that they opened the Bath the other day, and sent out a Commandry to the Admiral here. I earned that in the last war, and was promised it, and it was not well they did not include me when two of my own profession got it.

"No tidings even that the Government of this country is disposed to treat for peace, though it has been worsted everywhere, and has seen half its territory go from it; for the Pegue portion is ours, and the people living quietly under us, keeping large and well-provided bazaars.

"It is a happy reflection that we have in England such steady and sensible friends as . . . . and . . . . . Lord . . . . .'s defence of me was handsomely done, and his doing it at all was a generous act. The Indian press tries hard to find all the fault it can, and is catered for by some correspondents in the force; but they cannot get at much. No one ever thinks of troubling me with his opinion, unasked, and I consult only the heads of departments; so that the letter-writers deal mostly in idle conjectures, and these will never hurt me.

"There has been a very successful reconnaissance up the river, under Lieutenant Tarleton, as high as Prome. I am not sure, however, but that such demonstrations, considered in their results, may not do as much harm as good—to advance and then come away encourages concentration, of which the reconnaissance knows nothing. But as I am situated here, there are many things—such as the Indian forces, and the so-called 'co-operation of the Sister Service'—which give me plenty to consider of before I act."

Bearing in mind the clear instructions with which I had been provided, and the indisposition of the Government of India to become implicated in extensive military operations in Burmah, the force sent there under my command had at this time accomplished quite as much as had ever been anticipated of it, and quite as expeditiously.

The force reached the Rangoon river on the 2nd of April.

Martaban was taken on the 5th, and was garrisoned on the 8th.

The operations against Rangoon commenced on the 11th. It was assaulted on the morning of the 14th and captured.

Bassein was taken on the 19th of May; Pegue on the 4th of June.

On these several occasions the loss to the Burmese in specie, military stores of all sorts, including sulphur and saltpetre, was considerable. The guns taken were as follows :—

MARTABAN.

Iron. 1 6lb. Gun Brass. 1 3lb.
      1 3lb.   2 1½lb.
      8 Wall-pieces
                                    Total . . . 13

RANGOON.

Iron. 2 3lb.
      9 18lb.
      3 18lb. Cannonades
      2 12lb.   ,,
      6 9lb. Guns
      13 6lb.   ,,
      11 6lb. Cannonades Brass. 2 3lb. Guns
      11 3lb. Guns   5 6lb.   ,,
      7 2½lb. ,,   3 4lb.
      2 2lb.   13 3lb.
      11 1½lb.   3 2½lb.
      82 Wall-pieces   9 1½lb.
                                    Total . . . 194

BASSEIN.

Iron. 54 Guns
      32 Wall-pieces
                                    Total . . . 86

PEGUE..

Iron. 6 Guns   Brass 2
      10 Wall-pieces
                                    Total . . . 18
                                    ─────────
                                Grand Total . . . 311

The Burmese Government had been deprived of the means of resisting us in this quarter; and this service, so effectually done, had to be performed under the intense heats which precede the monsoon. To the personal attacks which at this time assailed me, as well as to the disparaging tone by which it was sought to undervalue the service of this noble and devoted force, I will only quote the words of the Governor-General in his Minute to the Secret Committee of June 30th, 1852.

"*Such is the actual condition of affairs at the present*

time in Pegue. Such is the issue of the expedition which it was resolved to send against Burmah. The most complete success has attended every military operation. A severe blow has been promptly struck. The three first cities in the Burman kingdom next to the capital have been taken. The whole sea-board of Burmah is in our possession. The trade of the country, both external and internal, has been stopped. The troops have achieved all this, now as ever, with a spirit that does honour to their nation."

In the same Minute the Governor-General says that "ample opportunity has been given for the consideration and transmission of overtures of peace by the Court of Ava, in the two months which have purposely been suffered to elapse, without any further political movement on the part of the Government of India." The policy which the Governor-General had determined to recommend, on a careful consideration of the several courses open to him, is contained in the same document: it was, "that the Province of Pegue, extending somewhat above Prome, should be permanently occupied as British territory;" and "that we should confine our military operations against the Burmese to driving them before us out of every part of the Province of Pegue, and then occupying it with the declared intention of holding it permanently, without proceeding onward to the capital."

Rangoon, July 31, 1852.

"All our operations in this country now depend on the policy of the Government at home, and we cannot get its decision till September. The Governor-General is here. He has come to *talk* on Burmese affairs, for correspondence is interminable. He is more than gratified at the state of the troops and garrison; and says, 'How we got into this place he cannot imagine, now that he has seen it.' By the capture of these works we neutralised all they had been about for eleven years; yet newspaper abuse is all we have got."

Rangoon.

"I have been very busy with the visit of the Governor-General. I had a house put in order for him. He was expected on the 21st, but did not arrive till the 27th. He was saluted by the *Fox* frigate and the Pagoda. I went on board with the Staff as soon as the steam-frigate anchored; and it is impossible for any man to have been received more kindly than I was. I arranged about the landing on the following morning. The next day (28th), at seven A.M., I was at the wharf with the Staff and heads of departments. The troops were all out, forming a street, the two ranks facing inwards, commencing at the Bund, and ending at the south steps of the Pagoda; the steps were lined with the Sappers, and the Artillery was drawn up on the upper terrace, a distance of one mile. A guard of honour, with the band of the 18th Royal Irish, was at the wharf. The Governor-General landed under a salute from the frigates and steamers. He had brought a horse with him from Calcutta, and, having mounted, we proceeded in due form and order through an immense concourse of Burmese and all Eastern nations for about a mile, as far as the entrance to the Bund, or fortified wall. Rockets signalised, as the Governor-General approached the gate, that the Pagoda might salute as he entered the cantonment. Here began the street of troops, up which we rode; the band of each regiment playing as we reached its flank—the men presenting arms. The troops looked admirably healthy and neat. It was a beautiful sight; and his Lordship was constantly expressing his pleasure as we rode along. On reaching the steps to the Pagoda we dismounted, and walked up on the platform; at top, Lord Dalhousie was saluted by the Bengal and Madras Artillery, as another guard of honour. We then went all over the Pagoda, and had a look at the east steps, where we had stormed in. He was surprised how the place had been taken. The upper terrace of the Pagoda is a fine open area, and the views from it wide and extensive. Having looked round, we descended the south steps, remounted, and rode to breakfast; and in the evening I had a dinner-party of seventeen, and so each day. I hope and believe that I did not leave anybody out."

"*Sunday.*—Church. At one, his Lordship had a levee; and at two he re-embarked under salutes.

"We have a population here of 70,000 people: Burmese, Armenians, Chinese, and people, seemingly, from all parts of India. The place is under military law; but this affects very few: personal punishment is very mild, and very seldom inflicted. The only serious offence with me is that of selling liquor to the soldiers—that I never forgive. I always hear the case myself; and the sentence is transportation to Moulmein, families and all. I sent seven, a merchant as he called himself, an Armenian, at their head, soon after our occupation of this place, and I have only had one man to deal with since. This is the most regular army I ever was with; but I fear spirits far more than I do Burmese. Its health is now admirable; and it wants for nothing in the shape of wholesome food. In this mixed force—composed of Bengalese, and Madrasees, with institutions as different as Prussians and Austrians—all has been harmony, and I have had no trouble whatever. The order is such as to have surprised Lord Dalhousie. The population is quiet, and I have not had a complaint against a single soldier."

Rangoon, same date.

"I was much taken up during the Governor-General's visit. I am glad that he came, as we have arranged and mutually understood many important matters which letters could never have done so well. Lord Dalhousie, too, was much gratified, and constantly expressed himself in terms of warm admiration of the troops, their noble order, health, and strength.

"Our future operations will depend on the instructions from home; and what these may be will not be known till September. It is hoped and expected that the lower country or Pegue may be annexed—in feeling and disposition it is already ours; and I only hope that the same merciful considerations will guide the Home Government which has actuated that of India, but somehow I *fear* it. Policy alone will direct it. Should this country not now be annexed, a shocking tragedy will be enacted over again here; to annex would eventually end the war, as our occupation of Prome would be the end of our progress. This policy would give us a most productive country, and, perhaps, would be the cheapest mode of proceeding. The moral effect in India might, perhaps, be against us; and we might have troublesome neighbours, and be obliged to march on Ava after all.

"I have a fine reinforcement under orders in the two Presidencies in case the proposed policy should not be approved, and we should be ordered on; consisting of two brigades complete from each, in addition to my present force. I shall have more than enough for offence, but I shall have garrisons to leave of some 4000 men; besides, the distance is great, and it is as well to be sure of a respectable number after casualties."

Rangoon, August 15, 1852.

"I have little to tell you. I have been preparing for my move up to Prome I expect to hear in a day or two from Lord Dalhousie; he cannot, however, receive anything from home, bearing on the policy here, till September. From all I can get at respecting my own position and time, I may be in this country, with the Indian Army, two years certain, whether war or peace. If peace and annexation, which is the issue looked for, I may have a great deal to do, in forming and organising a native Pegue force. If peace without annexation, I shall have to hold that part of the country which is to be our guarantee for the payment of the money to be exacted. If no peace take place, I may have to proceed up the country, and in that case I reckon I may be before their capital by February, 1853. There may be offers of peace on our occupation of Prome; it may be when our columns are *en route*, or it may never be. In which case I shall have to move on; and if we assault the capital and take it, we must keep it and the empire, for we shall have no one in authority then to treat with, for the Royal Family and great people, with their wealth, will have taken flight up the river."

Rangoon, August 26.

"Yesterday I had a letter and my official instructions from the Governor-General. It is now intended that for the present our operations are to be confined to operations within the Province of Pegue. This is in expectation that the home instructions may consent to the annexation of this portion of the Burmese Empire; but which we shall not get till late in September, about the time my first 2000 men will have occupied Prome. There will be no peace by this move.

"I send you the Governor-General's order, and you may use it, if necessary, to contradict the many infamous reports circulated, to the detriment of this excellent force. Defamation is the sad penalty a General officer has to pay for serving in this country; but I bear it all very patiently."

MINUTE OF THE GOVERNOR-GENERAL OF INDIA.

August 13, 1852.

" Address to Major-General Godwin.

" Acquaint him that the Governor-General in Council, after having had the advantage of conferring personally at Rangoon with himself, and with Commodore Lambert, commanding the naval force, has, since his return to the Presidency, maturely deliberated on the position of our affairs in Burmah, upon the objects which the Government of India has had in view in reference to that state, and upon the most effectual means of securing the political ends it has sought to obtain.

"The Governor-General in Council has finally resolved that, under present circumstances, he will not direct the Major-General, with the army that shall be assembled under his command, to undertake a march upon the capital of Burmah.

"His Lordship in Council has determined that the present operations of the army shall be limited to the complete subjection, and present military occupation of the Province of Pegue, up to whatever point to the northward of Prome he may, on examination, find it convenient to fix.

"The attention of the Governor-General has long been given to the matter which is noticed in the Major-General's memorandum; namely, the means of rendering the flotilla in the Irrawaddy powerful and effective."

Shortly after the arrival of the expedition at Rangoon, Major-General Godwin laid before the Governor-General the grounds on which, in a military point of view, he objected to an immediate advance of the force to Prome. (P. 60.)

Of the two grave charges against me, for which I was held up as unworthy to fill the post I occupied, one was, that "I remained inactive at Rangoon during the rains." I had gone into garrison at Rangoon in conformity with my instructions; its occupation was to be the limit of our first operations. Had it been found untenable from a recurrence of the mortality of 1824, the force was to be embarked and taken to Moulmein. To enable it to maintain itself at Rangoon, every possible provision was made by the Government to pass through the monsoon in health and strength. Even before the force was collected together, or the officer selected to command it, admirable barracks had been sent round; slaughter-cattle had been collected at a very heavy expense; mills and bake-houses had been prepared, and which supplied the soldiers with better bread than I had ever seen served out to troops before. In spite of the infamous falsehood about the "measley pork," I never witnessed any body of men so admirably provided for. The great object of all this had been to maintain an effective force for any subsequent operations, should the first successes have failed to secure the hoped-for political results; and the plan had succeeded—no station in India presented a healthier body of men than did the garrison of Rangoon, or in more striking contrast to their position in the same place on the close of the monsoon in 1824.*

The responsibility of maintaining an effective force, and the risk of using a non-effective one, were mine; and why was I required to break up from Rangoon? Why was I to abandon all these advantages which had answered so well, as the returns will show, and go and take up an idle position in the most pestilential swamp that is to be found in the country, where I should have no cover for the men, and that, too, in the midst of the rains? Why change the soldiers from wholesome food, and excellent health, to put them on salt rations and biscuit? This was to be done for no earthly advantage; at the mere suggestion of a few weak-minded, or interested, ill-informed, and irresponsible persons; and simply because a few steamers had found their way up to a wonderful place called Prome.

---

* "Our situation at this time was indeed truly melancholy; even those who still continued to do their duty, emaciated and reduced, could with difficulty crawl about. The hospitals crowded, and with all the care and attention of a numerous and experienced medical staff, the sick, for many months, continued to increase, until scarcely 3000 duty-soldiers were left to guard the lines."—*Snodgrass's Narrative, p.* 79.

Rangoon, August 25.

"The naval affair at Prome has, I fear, seriously damaged the place for us, as we had intended to occupy it; and now a good deal of cover for our men has been destroyed. . . . The Governor-General in Council has approved of our remaining here during the rains—it was always his intention that we should remain; it would have been insanity to go where there was no cover—we should have crowded our whole force into hospital at once. The mere occupation of Prome offers no advantages: it is the half-way house, and a proper place for stores, in case we move on to Ava; but of this nothing will be known here for a month to come."

Rangoon, September 2, 1852.

"Every department has been, and still is busy getting ready for our advance on Prome, which will then become our 'head-quarters;' this place, however, will still continue our base for supplies of every kind. I hope to have my advance, consisting of 2,300 men, on board by the 18th, and by the beginning of November to have moved up as many as 6000 of all arms. I told you that possibly our operations might be confined to the Province of Pegue; from what the Governor-General told me, his hands will be loosed by the first or second mail of this month.

"No opportunity is lost, I see, of detracting from the merits of this force. You may take my word for it, that there never was an army in the field, or in quarters, which ever exceeded this one in discipline, order, and consequent health; no force in India has so few deaths, or so few in hospital. I sent you in my last Lord Dalhousie's order on quitting this place after his visit, and it fell short of what he desired; for he said that 'he could not do justice to what he saw.'

"The barefaced falsehoods respecting the 'measley pork,' and the 'badness of the rations,' were sure to be laid hold of; all this was aimed against the Governor-General as being concerned in the equipment. Again, as to the cholera, 'contracted by the men from laying in a swamp'—first, the men never lay in a swamp; but I should like to know how many swamps, and consequently hospitals filled with cases of rheumatism and dysentery, had we in the Peninsula. The ground had been burnt as hard and as dry as a brick—this I know, for I lay on it. Young gentlemen who don't like to take the ground now and then have mistaken their trade. The cholera was not contracted here, but was brought from Madras by the 51st Light Infantry and the Artillery—they were dying of it there; they died of it on the passage to Rangoon; and both corps got rid of it here. This army is in as beautiful order and health as it could be under the wonderful management of its detractors.

"A great deal, I have no doubt, has been said after all this writing, on my not having advanced on Prome. Had the occupation of this place been considered a matter of urgency, I ought to have been sent there at once; but it was never intended by the Government; and, when once established at Rangoon, I would never have listened for an instant to any plan for breaking up during the rains. The advance of the steamers to Prome was urged merely for an effect. There has been a great deal of very silly writing on the importance of the possession of Prome. It is of no use whatever, except as a second place to base our future operations on against Ava. It is with respect to the cover for the troops which we shall now find there that I am in some anxiety. I lived there for eight months—there was hardly any then; and I much fear that the fire from the steamers may have made it less. This act has vexed the people who before were well-disposed to us. If Pegue is to be annexed, the Burmese must be driven out of it, without any wanton destruction of property.

"There are posts of the enemy of from 3000 to 8000 about

this lower country, which, from the nature of the ground, we cannot reach during the rains; but they could reach us, and though had I reduced this force to 2000 or 3000 men, it might have held its own ground, yet a demonstration against it, such as that against Martaban, would have been most disastrous. The Talein population of this place is some 60,000 men, women, and children; all of whom would be driven in, in the event of an attack by the Burmese, under the guns of a reduced garrison, and the panic would be dreadful. Now, with a respectable force here, should they dare to concentrate and approach, as they did in the last war, I could meet them and chastise them if they waited. Reinforcements will put all this to rights, and enable me to move; *but I shall have some difficulty in getting a very small force to Prome."*

September 7.

" I last night received an intimation from Madras, brought by a vessel with troops, that the Fusilier European regiment could not embark, as it had a severe attack of cholera; so, you see, we might have had it again from that Presidency, without the ' swamps and the exposure.' *September* 12.—This leaves to-day. I am in full preparation, as are the regiments I have selected to go with me. They are delighted. My greatest trouble has been to satisfy the hopes and expectations of all; for all cannot be employed at once."

Rangoon, September 13—22, 1852.

" One regiment is off, to remain in the Irrawaddy for the remainder and myself. As the great steamers cannot cross the bar, the smaller ones take the troops to them; and the trip takes nearly three days. After I have settled the first 2000 at Prome, I shall return here, where I have a great deal to do. *September* 20.—This day concludes my first year in the East—a busy, eventful one to me. This time last year we were talking of Umballa and its beautiful climate. With how little certainty can we ever look forward! I had named this day to embark myself, but I shall not be able. It is a very tedious affair getting all these steamers loaded, together with the myriads of boats. We shall have a long, creeping passage up."

October 3, 1852.

"In the Irrawaddy, thirty miles above Henseda, where in the last war I had a brigade to hold the country, and enable Sir A. Campbell to cross the army from the left to the right bank from Sarawak.

"We are aground since yesterday morning, and, after herculean exertions, are not off yet; but hope encourages us, that in a few hours we may be again paddling upwards. Another steamer is fast, like ourselves, on the opposite bank. I hardly expect to be on the move with the whole flotilla before Tuesday morning. I left Rangoon on the 25th, but part of the force commenced their embarkation ten days before. The Admiral came into the Rangoon river a short time since, and is up near Prome, waiting to see our operations there.

"Since I have been on the Irrawaddy, I have received a letter from the Governor-General, full of care for this force, and sending reinforcements. The rains are a good deal over, but it is hot during four or five hours in the day. I have eight steamers creeping up, with myriads of boats, protected by a great number of men-of-wars'-boats, and a few schooners in tow. 7000 men and 900 horses will have got up by December. Any operations above Prome must be by land, with a shallow-draught flotilla on our flank; for this creeping work will never do. 150 elephants are crossing the pass from Arracan; so that I shall be a free agent on shore in case we proceed to Ava, which I think we shall have to do."

Prome, October 11, 1852.

"I will afford a few minutes for a few lines; but I am busily occupied in writing or receiving on business, as I leave this for Rangoon to-morrow. On Saturday, the 9th, we came to anchor before this place; each vessel, as it passed, coming in for a few shots. In the evening I landed about 1000 men, to take up our ground. The next morning the rest of the force followed. The heat here is intense, which made me land them in two divisions, evening and morning. There were some 3000 or 4000 men on the high ground, and about the Pagoda, and, I have no doubt, expected that we should attack them on the direct road to the Pagoda; but we landed at a suburb, north and beyond the town. The opposition from Gingals and musketry was at a small nullah, which separates the suburb from the town. This was soon silenced; and the enemy, seeing themselves turned, decamped and left us an empty town. I remained on shore."

Rangoon, October 15.

"I arrived here last night, and I have been busily employed with my Military Secretary, Captain Burne, all day. This leaves for Calcutta to-morrow, with my despatch relative to the occupation of Prome. My local knowledge was fortunate, as it saved the lives of a good many of our men. On the direct road they had contrived numerous hindrances; but having got on their flank, we should have driven them down to the river and under the guns of the steamers, had they waited."

Rangoon, October 22.

"We are all busy; no man, however, was ever provided with a better Staff. I am now writing to you as a relaxation, after several hours at it, and Burne (Military Secretary) hard at it too. It is dreadfully hot here through the middle of the day; but the mornings and evenings are pleasant. I never was so fagged in all my life as I have been since the rains ceased, or rather mitigated—now some six weeks. My pen is never out of my hand. I am generally six or seven hours at it; and in the middle of the day now it is a fatigue. Troops are embarking for Prome daily, but it is slow work. The river is difficult, and the steamers are constantly grounding and delaying. There is a strong force in that neighbourhood, which I mean to attack; *but I must contrive to get some carriage for stores for the days we shall be out.* I told you the present plan was to confine our operations to Pegue. I have always said, 'To find peace for Pegue, you must go on to Ava;' and I think that we shall find it so yet. We have got Bundoolah's son, who was threatened by his Government, and came over to our outposts at night, with only one attendant. From all I hear, this war cannot last much longer. The Government is in a wretched state, if there be any Government at all; and there will be more trouble in settling with them under this disorganised state of things than in carrying on the war."

Rangoon, November 3, 1852.

"Fagging has never ceased for the last two months. What with troops coming in, and troops embarking, together with the directing arrangements and correspondence relating to these provinces, I am pretty well worked up; and I sometimes get up to breathe, and walk about the room for rest. I am not oppressed by my difficulties, but it is the unceasing pen-and-ink work consequent on this war. Yesterday may serve as a sample. Up early; at work with the Adjutant and Quartermaster-General till one; receiving till three; writing to the Governor-General, &c., till four. I then inspected a beautiful troop of Madras Horse Artillery. I have been dining with some regiments, and the kind feeling shown me is most gratifying; but I am somewhat insulated here, and do not like it. But if this were broken through, I should perhaps be overwhelmed."

November 14.

" I am looking anxiously for the next despatches from the Governor-General, as I think something more decisive will be determined on than merely confining our operations to Pegue. I still think that to secure a peace which shall give us Pegue, we must march to Ava."

November 15.

"The last gun of 83 has just fired for the great man we have lost—one whom, if I am not greatly mistaken, some of us will sorely miss. It is a military calamity, and I sincerely deplore it."

The assistance rendered to the Taleins in the month of June had not enabled them to keep possession of the city of Pegue, which had shortly afterwards been retaken by the Burmese. It was reported to me that the several detached forces which had been moving about the lower country, ever since our first occupation of Rangoon, had re-assembled in considerable numbers at that place. I determined, therefore, to occupy it with a sufficient British force, in accordance with the instructions of the 13th of August, which said—

"The further measures which may be necessary for driving the Burmese troops out of the district of Martaban, and for completing the military subjection of the Province of Pegue, are left to the judgment of Major-General Godwin."

These operations took place in November, 1852, and the result was fully detailed in my despatch to the Secretary to the Governor of India, of the 22nd of that month.

Rangoon, November 26.

"I have returned to this from the occupation of Pegue. Personally it was a trying affair, from the country we had to penetrate; but you will read it, and, having written my despatch, I am tired of it. *I got through the work with no fatigue, though on my legs for nine hours,* and constantly called on to see to things. I lent my horse at the end of the day, and there was no riding before. I am shortly going up to Prome, to have a turn up with our neighbours there. Active operations have, I hope, begun again. God is very good to me in thus preserving me in such health and wonderful strength! Young men were much more fagged than I was, and under such a heat too!"

Rangoon, December 9, 1852.

" I did quite right in not breaking up from this; no one but a very ignorant man, or a very thoughtless one, would. The move has been too soon already, for that swamp Prome has given me a larger hospital than I have had yet. I do as I think proper; and no amount of detraction and insult will ever make me alter my course when I know that it is the right one.

"This is a troublesome war: we only want a force to go against, instead of one dispersed over the country, and engaged in worrying villages. At Prome I have been encouraging the enemy to get strength, by not noticing them, though their outposts are very near us. Sir J. Cheape, who commands there, understands this, and is acting well up to it. I have been much distressed by the death of Brigadier M'Neil, who commanded the troops under me at Pegue. He died of exhaustion and the effects of the sun, which brought on inflammation of the brain. I am going to Pegue again, where I am required."

Rangoon, Christmas-day, 1852.

" I am overwhelmed with writing, as are all others about me. You will see by my report what took me again so soon to Pegue and what we have been about. We had several days of hard work; if they would not fight, it was not from my not giving them a fair chance. In our pursuit of the Burmese the last night, I visited the picquets in a wet jungle; it was very warm, and I caught such a horrible cold as I did not think this climate could give, with fever—in fact, the worst influenza I have ever had. I am better to-day, but obliged to write and see people all day, and this knocks me up.

"On Tuesday I go to Prome.

"The Province of Pegue is no longer Burmese, but a part of British India. Annexation was proclaimed this week. I still think that we must go up to Ava if we want a peace. Our operations are confined to Pegue. I am disgusted at a good deal . . . and after I have given the Burmese force about Prome a good beating, I have serious thoughts of resigning this command. The course this war has taken has so disappointed me that I hate it, and shall be glad to get away from it. But we may see something yet! After this I shall be at Prome, where I have a noble house."

Prome, January 12, 1853.

"The war in this country is, I think, at an end: our work at Pegue somewhat accelerated this. There has been a revolution at Ava in consequence of the peace party finding itself sufficiently strong to declare itself, at the head of which is the presumptive heir to the throne. This has drawn up to the capital all the influential men who were in command of bodies of troops in Pegue and Martaban. What this political change has done, twice my force could not have done: it has cleared the country—all have moved to the north like so many flights of birds.

"This is a most fortunate event for the Indian Government, and some sort of a treaty may follow. It is too late for the new Burmese Government to think of holding anything except Burmah Proper, above Prome. The whole of the lower country is formally annexed, and is British-Indian. A proclamation, with a commission for the Civil Government, has arrived, so that this part of the question is all settled. Lord Dalhousie is a fortunate man: he has consolidated this marvellous Indian Empire, by giving it an excellent eastern frontier. We have a complete coast-line along the east side of the Bay of Bengal; it has put an end to the uncertain relations we have had with this restless people, the Burmese, ever since the last war, and prevented the establishment of a French or American power in these regions, either of which might have happened to us. The Home Government would not listen to the proposition of taking the whole country, but limited itself to the productive portion; and it has certainly made a noble acquisition. Its port will be second only to that of Calcutta; the teak forests will pay them well, unless exhausted by the present wasteful system.

"I will not conceal from you that I have had some things to vex me for these four months past; but, thank God! my nerves are not easily shaken. I have never departed from my determination, though I have had difficulties to contend with. I have ever felt perfect confidence that my course was right, and no one in the force or out of it has ever had any influence over me. This may have annoyed the Government; but every act I have taken on myself to judge for has turned out at least fortunately. I have been annoyed by the proceedings of swaggering, irresponsible people, who have not faced me, but written to the Government: my position here has stood in the way of interference; but a man who would have given way to every suggestion would soon have been a cypher. I have been very plain with everyone, and most likely to my own injury. I have never in one instance been pushed back by the enemy—they have been beaten on all occasions, and, what I esteem most, with little loss: to attain this has been my great object. Officers and men know this, and have confidence in me.

"People here even have been very slow to understand our true position: our ultimate object—the acquisition of the Province of Pegue, would have been much more effectually served by not disturbing the villages of the Taleins, and by not bringing on them the vengeance of the Burmese soldiery. Captain Tarleton's operations at Prome were a matter of necessity, and he is a most excellent officer; but I cannot help thinking that we should have had all the inhabitants with us when we came up, instead of which they had been driven away by the guns on one side, and the Burmese on the other.

"As to what you say respecting the newspaper attacks, I can assure you that, with reference to the English ones, my feeling is mainly one of astonishment that men should risk opinions founded on such imperfect information as their correspondents concoct for them. As to the Indian press, depreciation of a Queen's officer in command is too telling a topic to be foregone. I would not give a rupee to put a stop to it all; it has been overdone.

"I shall give up this army should a peace be the result of the commotion at Ava, and resume my division at Umballa. This war has been one of great labour and anxiety; but, unless I am very much mistaken, it will never be either honour or advantage to me. I came here a Lieutenant-General. I am now a Major-General, nor has my position here given me an additional rupee. I am told that the difference betwixt me and others will some day be made up to me. We shall see! The Governor-General said to me one day at dinner (at Rangoon) that there would be honours, but not much batta. . . .

"The story of my not being any longer a Lieutenant-General is just this. The last brevet made several officers of the East India Company's service, Lieutenant-Generals over the heads of Queen's officers. This the Commander-in-Chief set to rights, by issuing commissions of Lieutenant-General to such of those Generals as were in India. In this I was included; but I foresaw that it would put all wrong, for as Lieutenant-Generals we could not hold our Divisional commands. But the rank should have been secured to me for my Burmese command.

"I am well lodged here, in a fine large convenient house, part of a sort of Buddhist monastic establishment, and a noble one, in a large inclosure; and on my arrival here I found that the engineering department had provided well for me.

"This is a sickly place, from the swamps which surround it, and the mortality has been very serious among the European troops. *I knew that it would be so, and pointed out the objections to an occupation during this wet season.* We were full early, and it is quite bad enough as it is; but knowing what I did, I should have been unfit to command had I been moved by hints, or ignorant, impertinent observations, or the gabbling abuse of newspaper editors.

"In my despatch on occupying Prome I said, 'The Governor-General in Council was aware of my intention, at the proper season, when the monsoon here had in some measure subsided, to break up the army at Rangoon, and remove its head-quarters to Prome.'

"I had nothing to say as to the time at which the war was entered on—at the coming season of the monsoon; but I was determined to be secure against the consequences. *Before the monsoon had set in I had done all and more than had been contemplated by the Government, when the force was despatched; and after that I was resolved to take care of the fine fellows intrusted to me.*

"My health and power of bearing fatigue is wonderful, and it is the remark of the whole force that I could kill the youngest man in it; and God knows with what regret I have seen some sink, especially in the Pegue affair, which was the most arduous personally we have yet had. I was on my legs for nine hours, under a burning sun, through a country of high grass and jungle, where we could not see a yard. I never felt distressed, but when it was over walked about; and at night, before I lay down, I went round the picquets, to see the position of the sentries. I always feel fresh and strong. I have my horse led, and have generally lent him to some tired officer. But my portly appearance is gone; my face is now so thin that it would make you laugh. Do not fancy from this that I am playing the boy; I am too old for that. When there is no special work to be done, and no example to set, I take care of myself; but, thank God! I am a strong man yet, mind and body, and an independent one.

"Everything is carried on in this force in all its stations with such regularity and good understanding as to give me no trouble on this score. I have relieved myself of the detail duty of this station. Sir J. Cheape has it, as General Steele has Rangoon. I have only the calls of the army collectively, its various returns, &c. Each General of Division has his own complete Staff.

"For the last two months the climate of this place has been cool and agreeable, the thermometer averaging from 57° to 60°: early in the morning about 50°, and the day warms up to 80° or 83° for three or four hours.

"I am going with a force to Meeaday, about sixty miles beyond this; the column marches under Sir J. Cheape. Should there be no peace, we may have enough of this early marching soon, for I never count on anything certain in this country for two days together. I shall return after I have posted a party there, and shall be absent about ten days. I have been there twice before, and know all the country in the direction of Tongho well, having marched over it."

Prome, February 7.

"I have returned from Meeaday, having put a garrison, with a view to its being our boundary-line. It is a delightful spot, with beautiful scenery all around it, and our progress up the river reminded me of former times. To look at Prome, you would be much taken with its hills, wooded ravines, and fine though not extensive plains; but it is a most direful and unhealthy place. Our mortality here is most grievous. I knew this: we have cholera here always, and other bad forms of disease. The early mornings are very cold, and the subsequent rise to 84° is very trying to all; but there is something more than this, for I have posts near me and on the river where the men are in excellent health, so that the sickness of this place would seem to depend on some purely local causes."

February 14, 1853.

"I am only just recovered from a very dangerous attack; thanks to a clever man, and my own temperament, I am myself again. I was ill all last week, three days seriously so—cholera threatened. The weather is getting horribly hot; we have now 92° at three o'clock, the mornings a little under 60°."

February 18.

"I have an unexpected chance of sending this letter down, by the force I am sending to Donabew under Sir J. Cheape. A naval force has experienced a serious repulse there. I knew nothing of the expedition, nor have I had any official report. All I know of it is from the contents of a letter, from a Lieutenant of the navy who was there, to a Captain of the navy who is here. I have always told them that the Burmese would fight if you gave them an advantage. There were 260 sailors and marines, and 300 Sepoys in the background; they marched twenty-five miles to attack a position of the enemy, headed by Captain Lock, who was killed, together with Captain Price, Lieutenant Kennedy of the *Fox*, four naval officers, and sixty-nine wounded; ten guns, and 100 stand of arms left to the enemy. I deeply deplore it. Sir J. Cheape is going to see to all this, for I am not fit to bivouac yet—at least, so the doctor tells me."

February.

"With your letter of the 22nd of November, there came one from my good friend Sir F. S., inclosing a copy of all you sent me. I am hardly so impressed with what he has so well done as with the manly, generous way in which he has come forward. This is not a world in which such a hunted hare as I have been whilst here can expect to be protected; and I look on all that has been said against me as well said, since it has elicited such a disinterested act of friendship. I have written him a long letter, giving him an insight into my position in this country. I am rejoiced at what I hear of . . ., and most particularly so of . . .; he is the best-hearted public man that ever lived.

"*My conscience is clear—I have not taken one step I could draw back from; nor, was it all to come over again, would I have advanced to this before the rains were over: the state of things we have had here tells me that the men, at least, have to thank me that I did not place them here before.*

"It is strange to me that I should have been the subject of so much virulence; no one can accuse me of undue pretension on the strength of my command. In India I have had no intercourse with any set. I have never shown any undue favour to the Royal Army, but have meted out Staff-appointments more to the Company's officers. Without any feelings of this sort, I have endeavoured to be just; and it is considered, I believe, that I have been so. I have had no favourites. Being in the Queen's service, the press of India thinks to please the Indian service by making a set against me; but in my heart I believe that there is not a gentleman in that service who thanks them for it.

"Well, I did rejoice when I got the command of this army; but, from the trouble and annoyance I have had of late, I much doubt whether I value it any longer. The army itself has never been the least trouble to me—I have gone on with it as easily as with my own household; but there is an evident wish to see things in an unfair light, and I am going on with people who never approach me with advice, but who are listened to elsewhere. However, all they get is independent truth—no man will ever move me from what I know to be right; and this has given offence. My variance originated in an impudent interference with the departments of the army; all went on well up to the Governor-General's visit to Rangoon. . . .

"No man can gain any credit by serving a Government which lays itself open to receive *private* communications; to such a Government irresponsible people swagger as to 'what they would do,' and 'where they would go,' neither inquiring or caring a rush as to the means of accomplishment. Should the thing be done and succeed well, they get praised in the despatch: but should it fail, through want of sufficient means, provisions, carriage, &c., they would coolly say, 'Oh, that was the General's affair.'"

Prome, February 25, 1853.

"Matters seem tending to peace. By the accounts of to-day, the half-brother of the King has been successful in capturing the palace. The King himself is confined to the women's Palace; and his reign, it is expected, will shortly cease. The brother professes an anxiety for peace; and as he has all along been of that party, I think that he is sincere: but for this I think that I should have prevailed on the Government to have allowed me to march on the capital, as means of carriage was arriving.

"Yesterday 160 elephants, which I have been expecting for two months, crossed the river, and are now here.

"Our frontier, should we annex, will be from Meeaday to Tongho. This will leave them a fine territory still, but we shall acquire the greater part of the rice country, with the entrances to the rivers, and, of course, the ports; together with a fine tract of picturesque and very productive country, of much interest and rich in natural productions. Dr. McClelland has come here from India to take charge of the forests.

"We have accounts from Ava which make some sort of a peace nearly certain, though, from what I know of the procrastinating habits of the Burmese, I doubt its being very soon. In consequence of this service (in Burmah), I may return earlier than I expected when I left England. The war has not turned out what I first hoped, and I think that it is owing to the political changes and struggles going on at home that we so long remain without any decisive orders here.

"The envoys are expected down in about fifteen days, but it will depend entirely on their seeing their own way clearly whether they will accelerate or delay; *we have no discretionary powers*, as the peace is made at Calcutta.

"The heat is terrible just now, 98°, and increasing, but the sickness, I am happy to say, is on the decline; but it is a hateful place, and, as soon as we make peace, I shall move the troops to some other posts.

"I am glad to have the elephants here: the Burmese will understand it to mean that we are about to move on to Ava. I would that it were so, and that I were on horseback again! I went down to see the elephants cross the Irrawaddy; it was a fine sight. The river here is deep, and about 800 yards wide. They passed over in groups of from fifteen to twenty, their enormous heads alternately rising above, and then sinking under the surface. There was one obstinate one which would not cross; they re-passed two of the larger ones, who set to work and very soon convinced him that he had better go in.

"I have sent out a party of 150 this morning on elephants, four men on each, together with some cavalry, to *surprise* a Burmese near this. I don't expect that they will do that; but he has a good store of rice, which we want, and we may get that.

"This is a pestilential place, and will not be our cantonment, which will be near Meeaday, sixty miles higher up. Prome is very pretty, with its pointed hills and deep valleys, and is very likely to take with people as a station. It is surrounded by tamarind-trees, said by the natives of this country to be dangerous to live near."

March 3.

"The heat increases daily. What will it reach? it oppresses one. Last night was the first hot night we have had."

March 16.

"We are told that the envoys will now be down in about nine days; when I see them, I shall believe it."

A second charge against me was, that I wanted energy to march rapidly on Ava, and so settle the war, as a young and active soldier would have done; for this no epithets were too bad, no insinuations sufficiently insulting. My plain and simple answer to this is, that I was always most anxious and urgent to go there; and that I did not go, simply because it was contrary to my instructions; and that I had acquired the certainty that our operations were to be limited to Pegue, and were not to extend above Prome, as far back as the month of July, 1823. The occupation of Meeaday—a fine, healthy, military station, some sixty miles higher up — was taken on my own responsibility, and acquaintance with the country.

It was asserted that "owing to me 20,000 men were held inactive, crying out to be led to Ava, instead of dying in the swamps of the Detta." I should have been very much inconvenienced by such a force, and very much puzzled where to put it; but the statement was one which was part of the system of exaggeration and misrepresentation which characterised all the statements made respecting us. The truth is, that I never had more than from 11,000 to 12,000 men; and after deducting the several detachments, the casualties, from all arms, and the sick, my effective field force never exceeded 5000 men. With this I should not have hesitated an instant to advance on Ava, should the order have come.

Prome, March 27, 1853.

"Your last letters have given me real happiness, as showing me the interest you feel in the wish to put me right with the authorities at home—that *right* I will demand. 'Recall' me! Had I been unsuccessful, had I been beaten on any one occasion, I might have been so served; but I have invariably succeeded, and, owing to my local knowledge, have been the means of saving the lives of hundreds of noble fellows. I am taking no credit for following decently a trade which long habit and common-sense have made easy to me. I have always gained my point—I have never had a moment's doubt but that I should; my only wish has been to do so cheaply. No people know better than the Burmese when they have got you at a disadvantage, as they have shown those noble fellows the sailors on three separate occasions.

"I have put a stop to naval officers, be their rank what it may, ever taking on themselves the command on shore. I might as well take on myself the command of the ships!"

Easter Sunday, March 27, 1853.

"This day year we opened our first fire against the

stockades at Rangoon, and to-day the Burmese envoy has sent his letter to us, the Commissioners, and which we are to discuss and answer this evening.

"By the last mail I received a very kind letter from Sir Charles Napier. I was glad to see it, as some of the Indian papers thought proper to attribute to him the authorship of the articles in the *Times* against me. He ends by saying, '*I wish you all success; your job is not an easy one. You have done your work right well so far; and all that depends on you will, I am sure, be done well up to the last.*'

"The newspaper reading world is still, I see, told that I ought to be at Ava, *when I have never had power or authority to go there*. It has been my constant theme, 'Proceed to Ava;' but until the elephants arrived (146, not 250, as the newspapers said) I was helpless for want of carriage. I never felt anything equal to the heat of this place. I am now writing at 99°, and in some houses the thermometer is 100°.

"The attacks on me make very little impression, as they do on those about me; as all who allude to them do so in disgust at the intentional falsehoods on which they have been founded. The only vexation I have felt was, that the report of the *Bombay Times* that I was recalled should have been *acted* on till it had been confirmed, because the private letters must have refuted the invention. The inquiry was offensive, because it gave a presumption that such a step was possible. But, in the absence of all information, I wonder that it did not occur to the Governor-General at Calcutta to ask, 'What has he done?' My position with respect to the Governor-General has been not so much of the nature of a 'difference,' as that I have 'held my own.' *All difference, if such it is, has been the consequence of the meddling of others with what they had nothing to do*. I never will give way. *I should forfeit all respect for myself, should I have been capable of departing from a wisely-preconcerted plan, for the sake of humouring some ill-informed editors.* When a force is in the field, all must be subservient to the man who commands.

"Everything had gone on well up to the Governor-General's visit to Rangoon; when there, he could not praise enough the complete success which had attended the provision for the troops during the monsoon. After this, the Commodore got him to allow him to prepare the flotilla to take the army up and place it at Prome. I was kept in ignorance of all this, and did not know it; because his Lordship knew that I should strongly object to have the troops so moved at such a time. I therefore interfered; and, most fortunately as it has turned out, for this some hundreds may thank me for their lives. All this produced a temporary coolness, which has now passed away. The Governor-General is one to whom the country owes much; he has consolidated our Indian Empire, which has now a fine eastern as well as western frontier. The army, too, owes to him all the care and attention which has been lavished on it, and for this I shall ever regard him with kindness and respect. He is at the *head* of every department—nothing escapes him.

"It is vexatious to have to scribble all this to repel that disgraceful newspaper falsehood as to my recall. For every single act I have done in this country I would go before any military court in Europe, and prove that my successes have been well gained, and, thank God! cheaply as to human loss and suffering. It is for this last that I take credit. It would have been very easy to have lost 800 men against the works at Rangoon, had we attacked on the approach from the river. I might have done so myself, had I not been there before, and so knew the position of the place. I pointed out to Lord Dalhousie at Government House the very place at which it ought to be assaulted.

"Little did I know what was in store for me when I undertook the command at Umballa, and to go a second time to India. I am now writing in a temperature of 100°. I have marched through a whole day, and seen young and strong men drop under it; but this vile hole Prome almost beats me. Lord Dalhousie told me after Pegue that my bearing such exposure and fatigue, and then visiting the picquets at night in a heavy dew, was marvellous. Should we yet have to march on to Ava, they shall see what I can do.

"The interview with . . . was important. As to the complaint that I had 'allowed two mails to leave Rangoon without a word,' had the Governor-General only waited the arrival of the next vessel, all would have been explained: owing to a misdirection in the hour of sailing, my Aide-de-Camp was too late."

April 3, 1853.

"The ceremony is arranged, and we meet the Burmese Commissioners to-morrow; we have a good building for the purpose, and I am to enjoy the luxury of a dress-coat with the thermometer at 100°."

April 5.

"We met yesterday; and the Burmese Commissioners are sadly chapfallen. I almost pitied them. The ceremony of the meeting was a very beautiful sight. If I send this to-morrow, you shall have another letter when the peace is settled, as they have asked till Friday, the 8th. I hope that we shall succeed in this; all looks well at present, but I know that there is no counting on them."

Prome, April 9, 1853.

"I have only time for a few lines to tell you of the failure of the treaty. Our demands so far exceeded the proclamation that the Burmese Commissioners said 'that they were ready to conclude a treaty agreeably to our own professions, but that they would not sign away 100 miles of territory above what we had so clearly defined as the limit of our wishes—namely, the old kingdom of Pegue.' We had nothing to urge against this, and so the matter has been referred to the Governments of Calcutta and Ummerapoora. The use of the word Pegue was unfortunate; we should have demanded the cession of the territory we had occupied up to that time. The Woonghee, the first Burmese Commissioner, and Minister of the King, is a shrewd, clever, collected man.

"For the twentieth time, I have again urged, as the only means of settling this war, that, *to find peace for Pegue, you must go to Ava.* I am preparing for the move, should it be decided on at last, but I shall be sadly crippled for many things; however, I have excellent people with me, who will do all that is practicable. The disabilities imputed to me I know nothing of; and I expect that I could kill any one of my libellers by a mere trial of bodily fatigue. My mind is as clear as ever it was, and as steady as my hand, which never had a shake in it, and ready to tell the strongest of them the truth, as I mean to do after the war is over. I have thanked . . . for all that he has done; but is it not too bad that I should have to trouble people to explain for and defend me, who have done good service, without a single failure? Gross as are some of the attacks on me, I think very little about them, except at the moment they come before me; and surely truth, which is said to serve everybody, will also serve me at last. I feel wonderfully strong, and only hope that all this broiling will not tell on me after this is over."

April 4.

"The heat just now is almost unbearable, and it is working its dire effects on the army. I shall be rejoiced when this war is over. I now feel to hate this country—not for any trouble its quiet, tractable people, nor this excellent force, have ever given me, but for a good many other reasons. I know not how it has happened, whether from change at home, or the indisposition of the Government of Calcutta to take on itself any responsibility, but it seems to me that we have made a mess of it. All went on well till August (1852); and then, the first blow having failed to produce any political results, arose the question, What was to be done next? From that date there appeared nothing but vacillation, indecision, and confused councils. A proclamation of annexation is issued, and the initiative is taken on that proclamation for a treaty of peace. The Government of Ava accepts it, and sends down Commissioners; and when we meet and offer the articles, they are found to contain a demand for a frontier line 100 miles further up, including Teak forests and valuable territory. They refused to sign, and very reasonably, though I am most sincerely sorry that they should have had so good a reason. I should be very glad now was this war creditably terminated. All military interest in it is gone, and has been some time."

Prome, April 22.

"I should rejoice to be able to get away to sea for a month, but I cannot think of it. The time for our second meeting for peace-making is approaching. I warmly hope that we may make something of it; and thus enable us to get clear of this detestable place. Umballa will be a Montpellier to this.

"The country we have annexed is a most beautiful and productive one; and, I have no doubt, will prove in a few years, if well administered, the most valuable of our recent acquisitions. The Teak will tell well, and the Port of Rangoon will be second only to that of Calcutta.

"This is the only unhealthy station we have out of some fourteen. It is singular that it acts against the life of everything, even of our elephants. I am obliged to send them away into the neighbourhood, as I do the regiments, about eight miles down the river. It is not the amount of sickness, but the mortality which is so serious. Our loss here has been melancholy. It will not be our cantonment; I have settled that. I lived here eight months during the last war. We then lost great numbers of our men, but which we did not so much consider, as all was comparative at that time, with the frightful mortality of Rangoon."

April 28, 1853.

"We are now very anxious for the Governor-General's further instructions respecting the treaty. The Burmese Commissioners are still on the opposite bank. They have indubitable *right* on their side; we have the might to do as we please. The new King seems an excellent man—sensible and humane. Should the district beyond this be yielded to the Burmese, we taking the line east from Prome to Tongho, I think we may manage it. I have now a garrison at Meeaday, which I occupied shortly after I came up here, but as against the old King, not the present one.

"Should there be any discussion in Parliament on Burmese affairs, it ought to clear me, and do me justice for all the abuse and disgraceful comparisons to which I have been subjected, for not carrying on the army to Ava. Till February, I could not have moved five miles out from this, for want of carriage. Since July last, however, there has been no intention of going beyond Prome. On all questions of this sort, I am under the control of Government.

"All the posts along the Irrawaddy from Rangoon to Meeaday are in excellent health except this. I have a range of barracks on the hills above this. The situation is beautiful to look at, but has proved more unhealthy than below, and I have sent two regiments—the 18th Royal Infantry, and the 51st Light Infantry—to a place a few miles down the river.

"Had the Government listened to me, it would never have been subject to indecision; and I should not have been such a victim to abuse as I have been. The war might have been begun in September, 1851. If we had begun in September, 1852, we should have been up at Prome by November; but to continue operations during the rains would be to fall into the same error, with our eyes open, that our blindness led us into during the last war.

"This treaty has kept us here three months, though perhaps we never should have been allowed to move had we come in September. I am confident that it might have been over in six months, and that I should have signed a peace at Ava."

May 4, 1853.

"We are in hourly expectation of the decision of the Government, and we think that our final interview with the Commissioners will be either on Saturday or Monday."

Prome, May 12, 1853.

"I had anxiously hoped for a peace, and am grieved to say that there will be no peace: this singular people, with half their country gone from them, and that half by far the most valuable one, still maintain a haughty bearing; there is something very noble about them. After a month (April 9 to May 9) we again assembled the Tootoo. At the breaking up of our first conference, a letter from the Governor-General, depicting the delinquencies of the old King, was sent to the new King. At the last meeting we found that the King had withdrawn the power from his Minister—of signing a treaty, but had sent down a letter for the Governor-General, proposing to pay the expenses of the war, and not to forfeit any territory. In fact, the whole affair had been upset. We offered concessions as to boundary, but the Woonghee had no powers; so they are now all off, and I am under strict orders to hold the frontier as follows:—

"'Part 3. In the event of negotiations being broken off, and no treaty of peace being obtained, you will consider the instructions of the 13th of August, 1852, to be still in full force.

"'Part 4. It is still the intention of the Governor-General in Council that the present operations of the force under your command should extend only to the *occupation* of the British Province of Pegue.'

"I am then requested to make every arrangement for such a position.

"I still continue to repeat that we shall have to go on to Ava after all; but these last instructions are in accordance with orders from home. In the present state of their affairs, I do not anticipate that any effort to rid themselves of us will be made from Ava. For the present there will be a tacit sort of understanding as to mutual non-aggression, to be followed, perhaps, by a treaty of commerce; and so the present King will be spared the obnoxious act of signing away half his kingdom.

"I do not like to leave this army in the present uncertain and unsettled state of affairs here; but I am anxious to leave, if not this country, at least this place, for it is killing me. Had there been a treaty, I certainly should have done so. I am better; but the exhaustion from the heat and the pestilent atmosphere have prostrated me. No rain has yet come down to cool the air, and I begin to despair of any cessation of this heat.

"It is easy to begin a war with such a people as this: you may overrun their country and conquer it, but you will never subdue its people or Government by any process short of this, owing to their remarkable pride and obstinacy. Accounts come in not very favourable to quietude; and I keep to my old saying, 'To find peace for Pegue, you must go on to Ava.'

"From the day that I took the command of this army it has not, either individually or collectively, given me a moment's trouble or uneasiness; but my correspondence with Calcutta (which should have smoothed everything) has given me enough of both. I cannot hide what I think should be said, and I have lived long enough to know that no men are infallible—hence in the public correspondence, discontent, fancied neglect, and I find myself accused of 'tart language;' but in the private letters of the Governor-General, which are constant, there is courtesy, kind feeling, and full explanations : this is a curious contradiction." . . .

May 13.

"Now that all thoughts of a treaty are over, I am going down the river a few miles. My two Aides-de-Camps are there now. Some Poonghee houses have been put in order for us. I shall take some elephants, fifty infantry, and some cavalry, and shall remain there as long as this dry weather lasts. I also propose to visit the posts up and down the river. This change of air and active employment is what I much require, for I am not the better for the last five months' residence here. I did not know that I possessed a tenth of the power I have shown, of resistance of climate, exposure, and fatigue, bearing it over young and all sorts of men, who I see leaving this by every steamer on sick leave. I must have some good stuff in me, say what they may.

"We are all looking out for the first rain to lessen this heat, which is horrid : the glass to-day, 110°. If you wash your hands, the towels are *hot*, and so is everything you touch. The mattress of your bed feels hot, and you rise from it at once, disgusted. I lay on the cane-bottom, and that is hot too. No one keeps flesh here, and I am now thinner than I can describe. This place has hit me hard; but though so reduced in size, I feel such good stamina in me that I am aware of no ailments; my voice is good and strong, and my hand steady. Considering that I have come in for as much public abuse as perhaps any man ever did, and have had to put up with other annoyances, yet my position with this excellent army, and with every officer in it, has ever been such as to make it truly comfortable, and to my taste. My Staff is not only of men of talent, but true gentlemen; and I do not believe that any officer ever commanded a force spread over so large a tract of country which ever conducted itself more uniformly well than this.

"I have now been these two last days at a beautiful spot down the river. We have had a violent storm of wind and rain, which has cooled this furnace."

Prome, June 2.

"You will have had my letter of May 18, relating to my personal military position; all around this is perfectly quiet, and nothing further has come from Ava yet. It may be that it is too soon; but I should not be at all surprised at their total silence.

"I am now living at a lovely place, Nwamean, and feel quite another man. I am picking up again what I lost during the two last months of the exhaustion of Prome, sleep well, feel sound in the chest, and clear in the head. . . . I leave this in a few days to visit the posts, and shall be absent about ten days. All the heads of the General Staff go too; it will do all good."

Rangoon, on board the Indus, June 21.

"I find myself here rather unexpectedly. I was up at Mecaday on the 15th, to inspect that post. I had not been there more than a few hours, when two Burmese war-boats were reported to me to be coming down the river. They were shortly alongside, and contained the Secretary of the late Envoy, who had negotiated with us in May; he had with him three letters to the British Commissioners, which I had translated: they were official ones from the Government, written in friendly terms, asking for the Governor-General's reply to the King's letter, expressing every wish for friendly relations between the two countries, and in all ways speaking as if hostilities had ceased. The old man came up to me and offered me his hand, as an old friend. Some other business made me wish to see the Civil Commissioner, and I accordingly determined to run down to Rangoon, as I knew that the letter to the King had arrived.

"I reached this on the 19th, have settled all my business, and have got the letter, and shall be off again. . . . The letter will be welcome in many ways.

"The war is now virtually over, and time alone will show the success of the line of policy we have pursued; the army will be broken up, and some batta distributed to it. There is no enemy near any of our stations. The force here will henceforth be a divisional command, under a Brigadier-General. You will have seen "the Blue Book" ere this, which shows clearly enough how unjustly and infamously I have been abused, and that for having carried out successfully all my orders. Lord Dalhousie's paper to the Secret Committee (November 3, 1852) is one of the best, strongest, and well-reasoned documents I have ever read.

"My intention is to go up to Umballa, after leaving this country. I return to Prome to-morrow. I should have gone yesterday, but for the sudden illness of my good doctor."

Prome, July 4, 1853.

"This tedious drama has reached its end without a treaty, by a sort of mutual agreement to stop hostile proceedings. I consider that our position is just as firm as any treaty could make it, though I should have been better pleased had the signatures been affixed : the world would have been more satisfied with such a termination.

"Had my recommendation of advancing in February been adopted, I have no doubt but that they would have signed a treaty. Their signatures would doubtless have cost us a good deal. *We are as strong without it, as regards the Burmese; not so, however, with reference to any foreign power which might think proper to question our right here.*

"There remains but little to be done here. I am seeing to the efficiency of the various posts, so as to leave all well. I do not think that I shall at most remain more than six weeks longer in Pegue.

"There is a subject which has been inquired into which may yet cause some remarks, and bring down on me more censure than ever—it is the offering a price for Meea-Toon's head. The moment I heard of this, I laughed at its impudence; for no one in this country, not even myself—and I am first here—has any power to set prices on heads. It is very fortunate for those who did so that they could not make the purchase good. I should then have been forced to have acted seriously in the matter. Meea-Toon is as regularly appointed a soldier of the Ava Government as anyone we have contended with; he is, moreover, a brave, clever fellow; and had he been taken, I should have treated him well. Had I been down at Rangoon, the escapade out of which all this arose never would have taken place, and a great many fine fellows would have been saved. There was a hasty idea, like very many taken up here, that Meea-Toon had never been countenanced by the King.

"I am glad that the Governor-General's Minute (November 3) has appeared. I saw it copied into a Calcutta paper, accompanied by this remark, 'How gratifying all this must be to General Godwin and his friends!' But how can I complain; *I have only fared like every other man I can remember who ever held a military command, from the time I first entered the service."* . . .

Rangoon, August 2, 1853.

"These will be my last lines from Burmah, or rather, as it is now, British-Indian Pegue. You will read the particulars of the notification of peace and the breaking up of this force, which is now formed into two independent divisions. I embark to-morrow morning in the *Zenobia*: it was my intention to have done so yesterday, but I postponed it, in consequence of the station having offered me a dinner, which, of course, I accepted. My time was out on Sunday, the 31st, and my labours over, if I can use the word with reference to an army whose admirable conduct made everything easy to me."

Calcutta, August 9.

"Again at Government House! I closed my last hurriedly at Rangoon, on the same day on which the dinner took place. It was a beautifully got up thing. The room held 100. . . .

"All this was very flattering and grateful to me; and so I left that good and gallant army. For a year and a half every sort of appeal had been made to it, in order to beget distrust in me as its commander, as well as personal ill-will; and on this account such marked approval, respect, and distinguished attention are far more valuable to me than the greatest honours which could be bestowed.

"I arrived here on the 8th. I have had some differences with the Government here, and was not prepared for the kind and distinguished reception which I met with from the Governor-General." . . .

August 14, 1853.

"You will have seen that we have *assumed* a state of peace with the Burmese; but I believe that from the perfect quietude around our advanced force in Pegue, as at Prome and Meeaday, we are in as good a position as if they had signed the treaty. Such a termination would have been more satisfactory to the public, nor would it have been less so to myself to have put my name to it as First Commissioner. No war could have opened more brightly; but the opening was its only life and soul.

"Lord Dalhousie, in a note to me on my arrival here, says *that he wishes to be the first to congratulate me on my return, and on the termination of a service which will be more justly appreciated when ignorance and malignity have exhausted their influence, and time has further developed the result.*' This 'malignity' (a very proper word for what has followed me) puzzles me—knowing, as I now do, its source in that very Board by which India is supposed to be governed. I had always looked forward to an explanation in Parliament which should justify me; but there is far less chance of this being done now, when the author of all the malignity is connected with the Indian Government, than when he was opposed to the former Ministry, and his defamation was confined to the pages of a newspaper.

"It is strange to me that so much should still be said about steam after the publication of Lord Dalhousie's Minute of the 3rd of November, 1852, because he so fully and completely explains away that monstrous delusion. He says, 'It has been usual with the public press in India and Europe, and with many other persons, to urge the immediate despatch of a force upon the steam flotilla to Ava—thus to strike at the heart of the capital, and to terminate the war at once.'

"*Such a movement is simply impossible. The Government of India has not at its disposal the means of effecting it.* The steam flotilla is limited in numbers, and its operations are still further limited by the nature of the waters in which it has to act."

The voyage of the *Diana* steamer proved that it was physically impossible for our steamers to navigate the Upper Irrawaddy during the dry season. After a full exposition of all the resources of the Government, and of the courses open to it, the Governor-General sums up by saying, " The facts detailed further show that whether, disregarding every risk, the advance be made from Prome in the rain or in the dry season, the utmost amount of force that could be carried on the river alone would be 1500 men."

" I much wish that people would take the trouble to inform themselves before they undertake to inform others. A formal cession of territory, they may feel assured, was out of the question—it was what the King of Ava never intended to consent to. He said that 'he would never allow his name to go to posterity as having given away to foreigners the best half of his kingdom.'

" In the last war, Sir A. Campbell was authorised to proclaim Pegue British. This was done. After that, we receded, taking with us a crore of rupees—and a cruel job it was for the native Talien population. This King offered to treat; but when we met, money was offered: when it was seen that we adhered steadily to the point of the occupation of the country, it was soon plain that there would be no signing. In fact, they only thought of treating with us in the hope that they might buy off this last proclamation of annexation, as they did the former one.

" I have been thinking of returning home, and have been strongly urged by some to do so; for though I am very well, yet the work I have had of all kinds has been very great, and what twenty years at Umballa would not have been to me; but I have determined to go there for one year more. I will not expose myself to be told that I have gone home to fight for honours. I would rather learn in this country what has been done for us at home. We have given a beautiful and productive land, with a fine Port which may some day rival that of Calcutta. The former Burmese war cost thirteen millions. This one has been the cheapest which the Indian Government has ever conducted, and has not cost more than a million and a half: we shall see. I believe that, personally, no man ever thought or calculated less on what are called honours than I have done. I am not a favourite of Fortune; and, as yet, I have got very little for good hard work. I was promised the Commandry of the Bath, when the proper time came, for separate service in the last war.

"I saw Lord Dalhousie yesterday about the medals. He has strongly recommended it, and has done all for the army he can do."

Government House, Calcutta, August 27, 1853.

" What wretched malice to endeavour, by telegraph, to alarm the public, and do all that in the power of mischief could be done as to the proceedings of this war; and which, despite the untruths which have been promulgated, would have defied the finding of a fault, if the man who was intrusted with the army had only been allowed to know best what were his orders and instructions, and how to carry them out consistently with the views with which they had been framed.

" I see that the telegraphic report was ' that more troops were wanted for Burmah.' The simple and true story on which this exaggeration has been reared is this: A company of Sepoys, improperly posted at a place on the Salween river near Moulmein, was attacked by some insurgents, tempted, probably, by the position they had taken up. The Commissioner of the Tenasserim Provinces hereupon sent to Rangoon for some Europeans. My orders to the officer commanding there had been, 'not to furnish any troops without my sanction;' and had this order not been broken through in the case of the expedition under Captain Lock, that disastrous affair would never have occurred: the aid was given, the officer thinking that I should have approved. As the Commissioner did not succeed at Rangoon, he applied to the Government at Calcutta; and, to my surprise, *three companies* of the 2nd Fusiliers were sent to Moulmein: so much for 'more troops.' The said three companies arrived there long after the affair had been settled, were useless, and only remained there because their regiment was one of the reliefs, after the rains. Now, if anyone had thought for a moment, it must have occurred to him that the aid required should have come from the posts along the Sitang, where General Steele was with a good force. From this force the aid did come, and which settled the affair by dispersing the insurgents, even before the letter asking for support had reached Calcutta, *or before troops could possibly have arrived in time from Rangoon.* I received the account at Prome, and sent directions down to General Steele to see to the security of Beeling so immediately; and which were, to cross by the city of Pegue to Shoegein; *and the thing was done before the troops at Calcutta were embarked."*

Troops from India were never wanted, beyond those I first required. I never even thought of filling up the sad casualties at Prome; nor should I have asked for a single man more, had the Government decided on a march on Ava. And here let me explain, in answer to all the newspaper statements, that the service army in this country consisted of 11,000 of all arms; and that, had I been ordered on, I should have gone with a force under 5000, which I always considered enough; that, had I wanted more, I should have asked for them, which I never did, for I always had most readily what I wanted.

"As to the 'additional territory,' it is a beautiful and productive tract, extending some sixty miles up to Meeaday, which is a fine military post—a consideration which induced me to take possession of it before we had any offers to treat. The acquired territory taken altogether is a noble district—one-fifth less than the Punjaub; and when it recovers itself after the long fleecing of the Burmese, and has forgotten some acts not wisely done by us, will turn out a valuable acquisition. Had there been one commander, as in the war of 1824, all would have gone on better, and the disposition of the Peguees to become subject to us would never have been weakened.

"With respect to the position of Prome, whether in Pegue or Burmah Proper, and which is a point connected with the boundary-line we should have been entitled to under the proclamation, all that I know is that, during the last war, it was considered to be in Pegue: Trant has so placed it—many maps also do; but this, it is said, is our version as to its situation. All traditional and living Burmese authorities make it in Burmah. I have had a good deal of inquiry made, and it all tends to place the boundary of Pegue about thirty miles *below* Prome, near a place called Shamyooah—where poor Gardener was killed—and, running east, the line falls just above the Shoegein, on the Sitang river.

"The Burmese Commissioners were not very clear in defining the boundary; and as it is now understood that they never intended to *sign* away an acre of Pegue, the question is of no moment. We make Prome, therefore, in Pegue, as we do Tongho, which was an independent state before it fell to the Burmese.

"Everyone here seems to accuse the Government for not having protected me from the virulence of the press. For myself, I hardly see how it could have interfered: it might have contradicted, officially, certain misrepresentations; but I could have done so myself, had I thought proper. But I see no reason why this should have put a stop to the abuse. Though Lord Dalhousie's Minute has been out some time, your English newspapers continue to write as if I was the sole cause why British troops had not been led to Ava.

"As to . . . .'s idea—that, ' rather than have stood all this badgering, being in command, he would have pitched the Government to the ——, and gone on '—had I had carriage, I might have moved; but, for want of this, even he must have done as he was bid. After I had advanced to Meeaday, I said to . . . ., 'I think, if the treaty is not signed, of going on with guns and cavalry, with some light infantry, to Melloon, and so gradually higher.' This reached the Government. On this, the Governor-General, in a private letter, said, 'You are surely not serious in advancing beyond Mceaday?' and, by the same mail, a despatch came to me saying that 'no operations were to extend further on any account, as it was the intention of the Government to lay down its reasons in the event of the treaty failing—which was not considered of any moment.'

"I always felt that the treaty was an object, and that the best way of accelerating it was by moving on; but on reading the reasoning of the Governor-General on the value of treaties with such a people, and that a cessation of hostilities would be tantamount to one, I fully agreed with him, and do so now."

Allahabad, September 18.

"We are here after three weeks' journeying, and where your last letters overtook me. You say that 'you are glad that I am well out of Burmah.' I hardly say so to myself; but, since my part is over, opinions respecting it will be a source of amusement, and may call forth a full and proper account of it all. My position was one of much difficulty, responsibility, and annoyance; and I can say that no one ever heard me complain, despond, or lose my cheerfulness for a moment—no one ever saw me disposed to bend to fatigue or exposure. I was personally present at the capture of every important place—Martaban, Rangoon, Bassein, Prome, Pegue; and I never had a check. Whilst keeping in view the objects of the Government, I feel that I acted for the advantage of the force intrusted to me; and this makes me feel as easy and satisfied as if praise, instead of vulgar calumny, had been awarded me. —— wishes that I had never gone to Burmah: not so, myself, though I may gain nothing by it; for I feel that by my perfect knowledge of the country, and the character of its defences, I have been the means of saving the lives of hundreds—though even in this I was made the victim of gross falsehood and calumny.

"What vexes me most is to read, as I am now doing, such apparent ignorance, and such off-hand opinions respecting the country we have annexed, both in newspapers, and in the Houses of Parliament. One proposes that 'we should have limited ourselves to the occupation of the country on the right bank of the river only.' This would be to take what would be little worth having, and to give up the command of the noble river: unless we have both banks, all our steam-power could not keep it open for us; nor would it do to have to keep it open at such a cost. Another assertion, equally ignorant, is that 'Pegue Province is unproductive.' Why, its beauty, which so takes the eye, is all dependent on its natural productiveness, its magnificent Teak forests, cultivated ground with luxuriant crops, and meadow land with such grass as to keep the horses in the finest condition.

"You may depend upon it that in a year or two it will make a good return to India, as good as any part of the Peninsula for its size, and that Lord Dalhousie has acted with much judgment in the course he decided on. I may say this now without any appearance of inconsistency, though it may seem at variance with opinions I may have before expressed in favour of an advance on Ava.

"I should have been right as to going on; and the advance must have been made in the way and manner I had pointed out. This has been admitted. But the revolution, which drew off the whole Burmese force from the Martaban and Pegue provinces, relieved our Government of all its dangers, and rendered its policy perfectly successful, inasmuch as its military expenditure had been very small, and its territorial acquisitions extensive and valuable.

"The only thing I should have recommended would have been a delay of six months in breaking up the army—I would not have given any civil Government till after the rains."

Simla, October 15, 1853.

"There was some anxiety here for the mail of the 8th, as it was thought that it would contain the brevet and rewards for Burmah. I did not expect it. I have done my best to report on all who exerted and distinguished themselves, as also to obtain what I feel is *due to all*. I had some conversation with the Governor-General about the medals when at Calcutta; he has strongly recommended it, and I feel satisfied from all I heard that he has done all he can for the army of Burmah. As to myself, the last words Lord Dalhousie said to me were, 'In about a month I hope to write to you, with what will be agreeable to you.' From the day when I embarked for Burmah till now, I never gave the subject—of what advantages my position might bring with it, five minutes' thought. I may have been disappointed at finding myself the subject of falsehood and calumny, when I felt and knew that my exertions for the order, efficiency, and invariable success of the forces I commanded were creditable; but I cannot be disappointed as to rewards. . . .

"I am quite content to remain as I am. No title will ever be so dear to me as that of my rank as a soldier in the army I commanded, and from which army I received every possible mark of honourable distinction, confidence, and respect—this honour no one can take from me. I know what I am entitled to look to: taking the rank of the Generals of Division who served under me, and the extent and value of the acquisitions of this last war, I have a *right* to expect what my old Chief got for the war of 1824.

"I find the climate of this place invigorating and healthy, and can hardly believe in the change to warm clothing, after the constant perspiration in which I have lived for the last nineteen months. I am regaining flesh and firmness in my muscles, which used to hang about me. We shall all be much benefited by our visit here; in the meantime, my house at Umballa is being put into order for me. I propose to leave this about the 20th, when I shall have a good deal to do in my Division for the next five or six months."

GENERAL ORDER BY HIS EXCELLENCY THE COMMANDER-IN-CHIEF.

Head Quarters, Simla, 26th Oct., 1853.

With deep sorrow—a sorrow sacred to the memory of rare private worth and recorded public merit—the Commander-in-Chief in India makes known to the Army the death, at Simla, after brief but severe illness, of Major-General Godwin, C.B., commanding the Sirhind Division, and recently holding chief command of the combined field force which achieved the conquest of Pegue.

Sir William Gomm feels assured that the Army at large will regret with him the sudden departure from amid its ranks of a distinguished soldier, a gallant leader, and an ardent promoter of its interests; while some, perhaps, will mourn with his Excellency over the loss of a long-tried and justly-valued friend, faithful and true from youth upward to the close of an useful and honoured life.

(*Signed*)   W. M. GOMM, General,
Commander-in-Chief, East Indies.

APPENDIX.

LIEUTENANT-COLONEL GODWIN embarked for Madras in 1822, in command of the 41st Regiment. In 1824 he joined the force under Sir Archibald Campbell, in which he commanded the 1st brigade of the Madras Division, and served throughout that war, having been present at every action, except in December, 1824, when he was employed at Martaban.

The attack on the stockades about Kemmendine is thus described by Major Snodgrass:—"The enemy's guns were for some time well served, but they were ultimately silenced by the superior fire from the shipping; and at the preconcerted signal of 'breach practicable' being displayed from the mainmast of the senior officer's ship, the troops destined for the assault, consisting of details of H.M. 41st and 17th Madras Native Infantry under Colonel Godwin and Major Wahab, pushed across the river, and, notwithstanding the stakes and other obstacles they had to encounter in landing, in a very short time surmounted every difficulty, the enemy suffering severely in killed." In the report of Sir A. Campbell, who was present, he says, "I now ordered Colonel Godwin to re-embark with the detachment of the 41st, and attack the second stockade, which was immediately carried in the same style."

In the course of the operations in Burmah in 1824-25, Colonel Godwin was employed in six separate commands.

70   APPENDIX.

The Siamese having assembled in force, and with uncertain intentions, on the Martaban frontier, Sir A. Campbell determined on taking possession of that province and town: this service was intrusted to Colonel Godwin. The force reached the Martaban river on the 27th of October, 1824. On the evening of the 29th the enemy opened their fire, which was returned during the night by the guns of the flotilla. At five A.M. of the 30th a division, consisting of a portion of H.M. 41st and 3rd Madras Native Infantry, were in their boats. "The attack was made under a heavy fire of all arms; but from the men getting on shore there was not a halt till they had possession of the place." 16 guns, 100 wall-pieces, 500 muskets were taken, together with great quantities of ammunition, of which the place contained a manufactory. Yeh subsequently surrendered without resistance.

By the capture of these places, and the voluntary submission of the whole of the Tenasserim coast, " the British," says Captain Marshall, " obtained possession of large stores of grain, ammunition, and ordnance, together with numerous boats fit for the conveyance of troops, and the command of all the Burman sea-coast, from Rangoon to the eastward—a district afterwards ceded by treaty."

In the General Order issued by the Governor-General in Council in 1826, this service is thus noticed:—"*Amongst those zealous and gallant officers, some have been more fortunate than others in enjoying opportunities of performing special services. The ability with which Colonel Godwin of H.M. 41st achieved the conquest of the fortified towns of Martaban and its dependencies appears to confer on that officer a just claim to the separate and distinct acknowledgments of the Governor-General in Council.*"

Previous to the advance on Ava in 1825, it became necessary to open a passage up the Lyne river, the entrance to which was commanded by the Burmese, who were strongly stockaded at Than-ta-Bain. The naval force was under Captain Chads, R.N.; and Colonel Godwin, who had just returned from Martaban, was appointed to the force destined to attack. "On arriving before the works," says Captain Trant, "the Colonel summoned the Chief to surrender, who required a delay of three days. This was inadmissible; and our troops advanced to the assault with such celerity that the fire of thirty pieces of cannon passed over them." Thirty-six mounted guns were taken; and an immense number of fire-rafts, filled with combustibles for the annoyance of the shipping, were destroyed. The Burmese were again attacked at Panlang: "thus entirely clearing the lower part of the country from the remains of the Burmese army."

This service was noticed as follows in the letter of the Secretary to Government to Sir. A. Campbell:—"I am directed to acknowledge the receipt of your despatch relative to the capture of the strong post of Than-ta-Bain by a detachment of troops under the command of Colonel Godwin. *The Governor-General in Council is happy to observe, in the signal and complete success which attended the operation, the same judgment, energy, and skill on the part of Colonel Godwin which distinguished his conduct on the occasion of his being detached to Martaban, and which again demands the unqualified approbation and applause of his Lordship in Council.*"

After the capture of Prome and the establishment of the troops there, Sir A. Campbell sent Colonel Godwin with a force towards Tongho, in order to tranquillise the minds of the people, clear the country of predatory bands, as well as to procure cattle for the army. Colonel Godwin returned by Meeaday, bringing with him 500 head of cattle.

The affair at Sembike is thus noticed by Captain Trant: —"The light companies of the column, under Colonel Godwin, immediately assaulted the stockade; whilst Major

Chambers of the 41st Regiment made a most gallant and successful charge at another point. The Shaans received them with a cool and well-directed volley, by which four officers and sixty men fell killed or wounded, and then stood to their works, with a determination to stand the assault. The bayonet soon decided the affair—300 Shaans and Burmese were killed in the stockade; their venerable General, Maha Nemion, amongst the number."

United Service Magazine
February, 1854.

www.ingramcontent.com/pod-product-compliance
Lightning Source LLC
Chambersburg PA
CBHW032133090426
42743CB00007B/586